莫小煊

Miss/Mrs Mo

林初 著

英国百科图书出版社
UK ENCYCLOPEDIA BOOKS PRESS LTD

莫小煊 / 林初著 . -- 英国百科图书出版社 , 2023.10
ISBN 978-1-915050-61-8

Ⅰ . ①莫… Ⅱ . ①林… Ⅲ . ① 文学 – 中国文学 – 小说
Ⅳ . ① I247

莫小煊

作　者	林　初
责任校对	刘　峰
封面设计	安　吉
出版发行	英国百科图书出版社 UK ENCYCLOPEDIA BOOKS PRESS LTD
地　址	英国伦敦切斯赛德商务中心切斯赛德路 39-41 号 CHASE BUSIENSS CENTER 39-41 CHASE SIDE LONDON
开　本	1/32
尺　寸	140mm*210mm
印　张	4.75
字　数	69 千字
版　次	2023 年 10 月第 1 版
印　次	2023 年 10 月第 1 次印刷
书　号	ISBN 978-1-915050-61-8
定　价	5.00 英镑

人还是要经常面对黑暗，

不然就无法学会捕捉光明

Contents / 目　录

1. 恨嫁女

莫小煊是我的高中同学，其实高中的时候我们没有太多的交集，但意外的是从上大学到步入工作的这许多年，我们一直保持着联系，虽然是有一搭没一搭地聊着，但是竟成了陪跑彼此最久的朋友之一，谈不上是知己，可也算是能够彼此分享心事的人。

然而我和她的性格完全不同，我有些内敛，喜欢一个人的安静，可她天生风风火火，笑起来不仅声音洪亮辽阔，而且牙齿和牙龈也要全部都露出来。可她长得极其美丽，葡萄一般的大眼睛，鼻子比整形医院的模型还要挺拔标准，身材丰腴，皮肤白皙得像杏仁豆腐，眼神里总是带着少女的天真烂漫，一不留神喜悦就从眼神里掉出来，显得她调皮可爱。她很少去掩饰自己的情绪，爱憎分明，这样的姑娘，你若是讨厌她，三句话就聊不下去了，可一旦被这种性格吸引，就会形成一段相当瓷实的友谊。

她的仗义充满火力，愿意为了你爱吃的土豆冰激凌跑满整个厦门，碰到谁欺负你了她先出头替你伸张正义，坐在家里就收到从世界各地邮寄给你的特产，神经大条，性格火暴，但一旦她也喜欢你，便会对你展开她的全部耐心，笑嘻嘻地做着你喜欢的各种事情来讨好你。这样的姑娘尽管少些矜持，可谁又能拒绝她热气腾腾的好意呢。

我上次见她时，是在一家布满植物的意大利餐厅，餐厅非常大，室内栽种了很多热带的花草树木，还有一个清幽的小水池，我们俩选择了水池边的座位，旁边还有一盆大吊兰，环境清新无比，平日里这样的环境，她肯定忙于陶醉和拍照了，可今天她却一脸愁云。她抚弄着那盆吊兰已经有十分钟了，刷子一样的眼睫毛垂落下来，怕是对面的植物都嗅到了少女失意的忧郁气息。菜上来了，她点了一份沙拉，我点了披萨、意面还有一些小吃。

“怎么不开心？”

“我要减肥。”她用力地戳着那份披萨，好像和它有仇。

“就因为这？”

她看着我，眼神变得欲言又止，默默地叹了一口气。

“你就不着急么？”她问。

“着什么急？”

“结婚啊！咱都什么年纪了。”

原来是因为这个，我的心稍微松了一下。

“怎么你着急了？”

“我能不急么？咱都快 30 了，各种催不说，再老就生不出孩子了。”

我披萨都快吃一半了，她还在对面戳那盘蔬菜，不过已经放过了吊兰。

“那你说个策略，我们该怎么办。”我把小吃推到她面前问。

她撇撇嘴，大眼睛里还是带着调皮可爱，但不似往日那般无所畏惧。

“我跟你说，我都相亲快一年了，各大相亲软件，网站，广场角都去过了。”

“好有行动力，”我卷了卷盘子里的意面，“那你怎么还这副德行？继续相亲，找到真命天子。”

“哎！就是因为相亲相多了。”

“怎么了？”

“啥奇葩都有啊！”

于是她开始絮叨，大概就是在相亲网站上碰到了很多奇葩，比如车速狂飙的“大仲马”；每天微信开口就是莫同志的70年代革命青年；甚至和闺蜜不小心共同约会了一个资深渣男半个月。

“你说怎么办，我现在都疲了。”她终于拿起了一块披萨，开始吃人类的食物。

“还是找身边人介绍吧，网上不靠谱。”

“身边人介绍的质量不行，”她是个钢琴老师，在厦门有个工作室。“你倒是把你们金融圈的高富帅多介绍我认识些。”

我看了她一眼继续吃面前的意面，这么多年她不是第一次跟我提这个，不是我不想介绍给她，实在是她不符合标准，高富帅的审美，可以说非常统一，某校长的眼光引领了中国98%直男的审美，这个不谈，他们对性格的要求也很统一：温柔顺从，少些自我，看起来好驾驭一点。这些莫小煊都不符合，她虽然很美，但不是网红脸，并且性格过于生动了。

“我找机会吧。”我这样敷衍了她一下。

那一天她一直让我帮她出主意，当然我也没有更好的办法，我也不相亲，一门心思扑在工作上。好像到了我们这个年纪，甚至再小几年的女生都特别愁着赶紧嫁出去，但是这样的女生嫁不出的原因，不是因为没人追，而是大多数男生她们都看不上，而那种看得上的男生，身边又一堆女生，甚至一堆女神。并且现在的男孩子都十分的骄傲了，甭管他们条件是否够好，可是骄傲一分不少，而且很多男孩子事业上不努力，追姑娘不努力，颜值上很努力，既化妆又去整形医院，估计心里也想找白富美来的。所以这个时代的择偶标准已经非常统一了：颜值至上。

那次聚会结束我们就各自回家了，她在厦门，是个钢琴老师，在大学任课，还开设两个钢琴工作室。**她很优秀，但是并不重要，这个社会不会因为一个女人的优秀而赞扬你，而会因为她没有嫁出去而诟病你，**莫小煊的自卑正源于此，她未见得真的喜欢高富帅，也不见的需要人家的钱，只是高富帅是这个社会的“好标准”，谁还没点虚荣心呢。在我看来莫小煊不差钱，也很愿意为对方花钱，她向来仗义，可是如果真要她来买房买车的，确实又有些委屈。

我准备GMAT考试已有半年之久，可成绩总是不理想，我没有莫小煊那样急着嫁人，大概也是这个原因。不是说我有多么的独立清高，只是经常在埋头去做事情的时候，感到一种解脱，这种解脱是什么呢？那种来自世俗意义上的压迫，该嫁人，该生小孩，该怎样怎样的方程式一般的人生。我从大学时就被念叨这些问题，到了现在还是时常被念叨，可我总觉得自己可以做点什么，但我也经常怀疑，我工作虽然为自己赚钱，但更多的钱被别人赚了去，我结婚，成为别人的妻子，虽然孩子是我的，可最终是别人家的孩子，就连我都是别人家的。**如果真的要用婚姻来定义一个女人的价值，大概从生到死，她都不属于她自己，她所做的一切，都被冠以爱的名义，奉献给了别人，**最多留下一座母亲的丰碑，可是大多数女人连丰碑都没有，在青春脑力生育能力被耗干后，早早地被踢出局。有的时候你觉得时代进步了，可这种进步却让弱者更尴尬，而强者更骄傲。

有一天我正在复习GMAT，语法问题让我头痛，我是个擅长应用不擅长理论的人，因此口语极好，而攀登语法的山峰，却发现努力了半天都只是在山脚下。

正在紧锁眉头头痛之时，莫小煊给我打来了电话，接到电话的那一刻我竟然长舒一口气，可以和她好好聊天放松下了。可对面却传来了莫小煊激动的尖叫声，我差点把手机甩出去，接下来是她激动得颤抖的声音。

“我跟你讲，”她几乎没叫过我的名字，我在她那的称谓就是“你”，“我结婚了！”

这回轮到我尖叫了。

“啊！你不是刚从我这回去么，还不到一个月！”

“对，我结婚了。”

我哪里想听她的重复，已经急不可耐地想从第一节看到最后一节了。于是在我的逼迫下，她讲述了闪婚的全部过程。

2. 初见

她穿一件白衬衫站在民政局门前，紧握着 LV 包细带子的手心开始出汗，天气不算晴，灰突突的像是笼了一层纱。莫小煊葡萄般的大眼睛紧紧地锁住车来的方向，她的睫毛很长，眼睛的面积占了整张脸将近六分之一。白皙的额头、雕像般完美高挺的鼻梁上渗出了汗珠，目光中焦虑和不安似乎将天气都搅动得更加惨淡了。她低头看了一眼手机上的时间，抿了抿桃红色的嘴唇，转过身开始在门口踱来踱去。

“才三天啊！”不安加速了心跳，她和他认识了仅仅三天，还是在社交软件上。

莫小煊仅有的一次为期不长的恋爱也以失败告终，今年已经 28 周岁了，无奈之下开始了相亲之路。**接近 30 的女人对待婚姻的态度，就像深夜的末班车，再不拼命赶，就要错过了。**她频繁浏览各大相亲网站和社交软件，父母亲戚朋友介绍相亲的状态已经持续了有半年，各路“神仙”支的招也是有所领教。

她天生爱笑，而且喜欢大笑，因此看起来很外向，但是也很容易受到打击。作为一个五官端正的大龄剩女，想要找一个三观正的适龄青年，难度不亚于从众多的鸭群里翻出一只白天鹅，毕竟丑小鸭与白天鹅也仅限于童话故事。在几乎集齐了 12 个星座和 56 个民族后，她开始疲了，厌倦了像商品一样被匹来配去的状态，男人到了她眼里就像货物一样被分类贴标签放在货架上，再这样下去她的三观也要崩了，因此像个蜗牛一样乖乖地缩回到了壳里。直到 3 天前的晚上，她遇见了秦朗。

一开始，她也只是随手匹配，他的头像是个清爽干净的男孩子，说话温柔客气，非常注重细节，她发出的每一条信息，他都会认真阅读，然后不早不晚在适当的时候给予回复。正是由于这一点，开场 3 分钟，他便获得了莫小煊的好感。10 分钟后，莫小煊心里的小火苗就开始升腾起来了，她若隐若现地看到了希望，渐渐地伸出触角，想要往前再迈一步。

通过聊天，她了解到秦朗家在厦门有 4 套房子，爸爸经商，妈妈是大学教授，这样好的家庭背景也获得了她的好感。

“不要错过机会！”她心里暗自忖度。两人越聊越投机，秦朗温柔体贴有耐心，字里行间对莫小煊的关心无微不至。

聊过半天，她感觉已经沦陷了，嘴角不自觉地挂上微笑，于是那个夜晚她没有合眼，两人一直聊到凌晨四点。她勉强睡了四个小时，去给学生上了一堂钢琴课，上课的时候也总是在想和秦朗的聊天记录，微笑不知不觉就在嘴角蔓延开来，她第一次觉得上课的时间那样长，中途去洗手间都迅速地先翻开微信去查看他的消息，她觉得那颗心已经由不得自己了。

第二天，仍然是在聊天软件上，两个人便开始讨论各自的家庭情况，恋爱过往，事无巨细。

“好体贴细心的男孩子！”

莫小煊心里想，他关心她的每一个过往细节，甚至贴心地叫她宝宝，告诉她困难总会过去，他愿意疼她。这在孤身一人在城市打拼的莫小煊眼里，是温柔的炸弹，在她干裂的情感土地上炸出了爱情的蘑菇云，伴随着感动的泪水，屏幕上那个温柔的头像在她心里有着非一般的意义。

第三天，莫小煊整个人都处于亢奋的状态，觉得生活中的一切都变得温柔了，学生家长，水杯坐便，无论活得死的，在她眼里都充满了温柔。自己的生活有些恍惚，似乎一夜间就从冰冷的世界掉入了温暖的春天，幸福来得太突然，而且更令她意外的是，秦朗竟然很认真地问她要不要结婚。

“不如我们去领证吧！”

提出这个主意的是莫小煊，就在他们从认识到当下的第 68 小时 39 分 47 秒。

“你确定吗？！！！宝贝。”

秦朗的信息也没有迟疑。

“怎么？你不敢啊！还是不喜欢我？”

她发了一个撇嘴的表情，对方三分钟没有回复，莫小煊快要哭了，就在第三分钟零四秒。

“只要你愿意，宝贝，我随时可以做你老公。”

空气中很是潮湿，洒水车经过的沥青路面上蒸腾着温热的雾气，让莫小煊觉得小腿暖烘烘的。7 月的厦门满街的水果商贩，五颜六色，琳琅满目的水果就像夏天的图腾，热闹闹地叫腾着。远处驶来了一辆蓝色的出租车，缓缓地停在莫小煊面前，她咽了一口口水，心跳再次加速。车门打开，钻出一名男子，关好车门后，男子走到莫小煊面前。

“莫小煊？”

男子露出一个微笑，牙齿有点偏黄。他也穿了一件白衬衫，带着一副金丝框眼镜，眼睛很圆很有神，脸很小，看起来有点干巴巴的，身材偏瘦，虽然有些没精神，可看起来还是斯斯文文，干净清爽。

“你就是秦朗啊？”

秦朗点点头，莫小煊的眼角爬上一丝欣喜，旋即扑哧笑了，露出可爱的小虎牙：“和照片上差别不大，看来你还没骗人。”

秦朗的眼睛盯着莫小煊愣了几秒，仿佛还没反应过来就陷入到了美丽的漩涡，眼神像是看到了发亮的珍珠。

“你和照片不一样，”秦朗垂下眼帘挠挠头，“本人更，更好看。”

莫小煊笑得更欢了，发出咯咯咯的声音，她的脸颊涌起一片绯红：“嘴真甜！”

秦朗嘴角也扯过一丝笑容，眼珠在眼眶里晃来晃去，表情里带着激动，可是也有一丝古怪，他有些迫切地握了握她的手，从始至终目光没有离开过莫小煊。

“所以，你还满意么？美女”

莫小煊收住笑容，眼眶里就要溢出泪花，心脏也要冲出胸膛，巨大的激动让她忽略了任何细节观察，她深呼了一口气，尽量使自己看起来淡定些。

“嗯，”她点点头：“满意。”

“真的？”

秦朗的眼中泛出雀跃，就像刚刚得到了皇帝的封赏或赦免，他的手握紧了莫小煊的手，使劲一拉将她抱在了怀里：“你可真美！”

莫小煊的脸红得像五月的牡丹，白里透红，她觉得有些眩晕。“那咱们进去吧。”秦朗松开莫小煊的肩膀看着她的脸说：

“现在后悔还来得及。”他看着莫小煊露出一个调皮的坏笑。

“切！”莫小煊推了秦朗一把：“怎么你后悔了？”

秦朗二话没说拉起莫小煊的手便往民政局里走。莫小煊心咚咚地在胸膛里打鼓，她看着秦朗的背影，觉得有些不真实：我要领证了！欣喜，激动，不安，雀跃，忐忑，期待，各种乱七八糟的情绪袭击了大脑，让她此刻有些麻木地失去了思考：我快 30 了，等不起了；我要把握住机会，不能错过好男孩；为什么不能闪婚？这样也很浪漫哦！各种各样的想法、猜测、幻想充斥在脑海中，可她的脚步却一步也没迟疑。

“咣”的一声，章盖好了，两个人白衬衫的照片在结婚证上显得十分登对。

“恭喜啊！”民政局办事员笑容满面地递来祝福：“下一对！”

秦朗拉着莫小煊的手，看着她的眼神就像她是一个宝贝，莫小煊感觉自己也沉醉在这个眼神里，她享受着他的爱，觉得人生的幸福感达到了极致。

“老婆。”他唤了她一声，嗓音听起来像公鸭，可幸福让她略去了这些细节，他的声音在她的耳朵里独特又迷人。

“老公。”她也回应了他一声，露出一个迷人的笑容，莫小煊总是笑，可此刻她的笑容就像盛开了的牡丹，完完全全张扬了出来。

秦朗拉过她喜不自禁地在她的嘴唇上吻了一下，莫小煊完全失去了思考，感觉心里的什么东西落地了，踏实了，安全了，可是还有种奇奇怪怪的感觉在后面，她说不清。他全然不顾地在大街上吻她，让她感觉害羞，紧张又刺激，她挣脱着从他怀里出来。

“这么多人呢！”她推了秦朗一把。

“哦！”秦朗略微失落了一下，不过马上被喜悦的神色掩盖：“老婆！一会儿去哪吃饭？”

“听你的，”莫小煊露出一个欣慰的笑容，眼里闪烁着幸福和羞怯：“老公！”

以上是我的脑补，为了让读者更加有画面感我选择了这种方式呈现他们的故事片段。

“所以，你们就这样过上了小日子？”电话另一端的我看着莫小煊发来的结婚证照片，那日期还是昨天。“真的太快了，你让我缓缓。”

我有些佩服小煊的执行力，这个看起来娇小美丽的女孩，心里的劲头真是猛啊，友谊的基础上，我开始对她多了一分钦佩。

“那接下来怎么办？”我问她。

“什么怎么办？你这话问的，过日子呗。”

“那，婚礼呢？你们婚房买了么？什么时候要孩子。”问完这些我就后悔了，因为我突然感觉自己谨慎小心在莫小煊洒脱的行为前显得非常 low，可是已经问出来了。

“一步一步来吧，”莫小煊说，“反正先在一起了，后面再慢慢客服一切困难。”她的语音语调充满自信和对未来的期冀。我突然激动得哭了。

“你哭什么？”

“你太厉害了，果然幸福要主动争取。”我只觉得心里被一股炽热的暖流所覆盖，大概因为我和小煊都是感情热烈且真挚的人，所以一听到这种热血浪漫的桥段，便总是激动。

“哎呀，别哭，搞得我都要哭了。反正你抓紧吧，我已经找到幸福了。”

那个电话我们聊了 2 个多小时，挂了电话后很久我都难以平复心绪。

我想人生是什么呢？婚姻又是什么？似乎我们都被一种无可名状的感情所牵引，莫小煊的结婚在我看来有些稀里糊涂，但是我也不得不佩服她的雷厉风行，**有些人总是要等到想好的那一天再做决定，于是拖呀磨的，可是想好的那一天到底在哪里呢？很多事情即便现在想，明天想，明年想，可能都想不好，甚至因为犹豫而丧失了许多机会，而我的朋友莫小煊，她不给犹豫滋生的空间。**

后面的生活遇到问题，大不了见招拆招，这闪婚，到底是幸福的天秤，还是婚姻的枷锁都不好说，可她勇敢地迈出一步了，而我只能在彼岸的另一头为朋友祈祷。

与此同时，家里人也不停地催促我的婚姻，用我妈的话来说：“家里的户口本我也不偷，外面的男孩子也不带回来一个。”不过即便她着急，也不建议我像莫小煊那样，她对莫小煊事件是极为震惊的，说苦日子在后面呐！因为她的态度，我还和她吵了一顿，说她不懂年轻人的想法。

“我是不懂，”她忿忿地说，“可就算买个房子还要看个一年半载。那可是你要生活一辈子的人啊！”

“土豪都直接买！看上就买。”我很不屑老妈的想法。

“对，你们都豪，总有一天生活让你狼哭鬼嚎。还不是我们这些父母来买单。”

我觉得这是一句诅咒，刚要义愤填膺地和她辩论，为我和莫小煊和自己争口气，她老人家直接关上房门懒得理我。

有的时候我也希望能像莫小煊一样博一把，怕什么呢？即便是精挑细选，最后也不一定走向幸福，也许小煊她正是深谙此道，精挑细选还不如大差不差，婚后再磨。这个时代离婚率太高了，**很可能再过十年，一个人离婚成了家常便饭，而一个人结婚会被人竖起大拇指称赞：你太有勇气了！简直是这个时代的勇士。现在的婚姻甚至不要和爱情挂钩，连稳定的合伙人模式都无法保障。**

但我还是满怀着热忱，希望步入婚姻的，只是冥冥中那个人在哪？我很好奇，但也不着急，幸而我总是很忙碌，忙忙碌碌中，也就忘记了这些人生大事的压力。

大概过了一个月我接到电话。

“什么？你们要离婚了？”

3. 他

离开民政局后，秦朗打车带莫小煊打车去餐厅吃饭，出租车里，莫小煊有点紧张又有点害羞地注视着前方，思想似乎还没有从刚领证的不可思议中走出来。秦朗时不时地侧过脸来打量她，手不自觉地伸过去握住她的手，莫小煊也回应地捏了捏他的手，两个人都没什么话，闷热的夏天，尽管出租车里开着空调，莫小煊还是觉得额头有些微微出汗。

车停在了人流不算太拥挤的一条马路边上，下了出租车迎面就是一家餐厅，秦朗付了钱后两人往餐厅内部走去。餐厅装修很有西双版纳风格，黑白花纹的地砖，土制的墙面上挂着五颜六色的版画，餐具上刻着富有异域风情的神秘花纹，这样热烈绚烂的装饰让心情瞬间升了个温度，莫小煊开始渐渐放下紧张。

两人挑了个相对安静的地方落了坐，秦朗细心地先把莫小煊让位到沙发的座位上，自己则坐在了硬木椅子这一端。菜单上来了，服务员站在一旁等待两人选菜，秦朗绅士地将菜谱递给莫小煊。

“看看你喜欢吃什么？”

“我都行啊，你来吧。”

“你来，你来，随便点。”秦朗憨憨地笑着。

莫小煊见状不好拒绝，便认真地在菜单上扫描，这家餐厅她以前没有来过，菜单上的菜品名字很别致：一道走在乡间的小路上，下面配图是红烧猪蹄；乌云遮日，紫菜蛋花汤；绝代双骄，青辣椒炒红辣椒；穿过你的黑发的我的手，海带炖猪脚。

看了半天，莫小煊指了指上面的一道名字还算正常的云南烤鱼。

“来个这个吧，爆烤罗非鱼，”她看向服务员，“少加点辣椒。”

“吃这个不会上火吗？”秦朗看着菜单摇头：“这种烤鱼啊，看起来挺大一只的，实际上没多少肉，还不好咬，能吃的部分没多少，而且大部分肉都干巴在骨头上了，不要点这个。”

“那你有什么好的建议吗？”莫小煊眨了眨葡萄般的大眼睛。

“你想吃鱼是哈，我看不如吃这个，”秦朗指着图片上的茄汁龙利鱼，鲜红色的汤上白色的鱼肉片显得鲜嫩 Q 弹，“龙利鱼没有刺，女孩子多吃鱼好啊！”

莫小煊看着茄汁龙利鱼 20 几元和烤罗非鱼 80 几元的价格，稍微停顿了下，旋即那种念头又被打消掉，应该不是图便宜吧！心底刚刚要泛起一丝不爽。

“不过宝贝，烤罗非鱼也可以，我来帮你挑刺，这样就不会扎到你了。”

“你好细心啊！”刚刚涌起的一阵怀疑被秦朗的这一番话给打消了，“还是点龙利鱼吧，挑刺太浪费时间了，那样我们两个都吃不好。”

“宝宝你怎么这么懂事。”

莫小煊笑了笑，略微有一丝感动。秦朗看着手中的菜单，指了指上面的一道青菜。

“给我来个这个，”他推推眼镜看向服务员，又看向莫小煊：“大夏天的吃点清淡的好，还有利于减肥。”

“你瘦得灵魂和肉体都要分离了！”

“嗨，不是说我，你们女孩子不天天把减肥放在嘴边，虽然你也不胖，正好，丰满。”

莫小煊拿起茶杯呷了口大麦茶，尴尬地将茶水吞了下去。

“小煊你看看再点些什么。”

“我都行，你来吧。”

“哎，别介，快看看，有什么你爱吃的。”

莫小怔手里握着茶杯，瞄着秦朗手里的菜单，服务员在一旁耐心地等待着。

“这个吧，”莫小煊指了指菜单上的咖喱牛肉，那牛肉看起来外酥里嫩，和红咖喱一起放在精致的小蛊中，看起来令人垂涎欲滴：“这道牛肉看起来不错，适合减肥，而且我也比较喜欢吃牛肉。”莫小煊抬起眼皮看着秦朗。

秦朗摸了摸脑袋，点点头：“牛肉是不错，但是它这图片上的料看起来也太少了，而且土豆胡萝卜怎么那么多。”

“抱歉先生，”一旁的服务员开口了，“实物和图片是不一样的哦。”

“是不一样，图片都这么少了，那实物还不得更少。”

莫小煊皱着眉头觉得更加尴尬。

“不是的，实物可能要多一些，拍照片的时候主要为了美观……”

“什么美不美观的，你们这种餐厅我来得多了，上菜的时候，没几粒肉全是蔬菜不说，肉我都怀疑是不是真正的牛肉。”秦朗转过头……看着莫小煊：“亲爱的，现在在外面吃肉可得注意啊，有些无良餐厅肉源不知道哪里来的。”说完还瞪了服务员一眼。

“先生您放心，食材绝对是真正的牛肉，肉源绝对安全。”服务员微笑着说。

“都这样讲嘞，我才不信。”秦朗不依不饶地说，“小煊你看看点些别的吧，主要是为了你的健康，你以后和我在一起，我一定要好好照顾你的身体。”

莫小煊的脸红了，一方面觉得更加尴尬了，一方面又觉得有些甜蜜，她再次喝了一口茶水：“要不，亲爱的都你来吧，你点，我不挑。”

秦朗点点头：“我觉得吃肉不好，我平时吃得都很素。”

“素菜我们也有很多，先生往后翻一翻。”

秦朗快速地翻着菜单，将菜单一合：“给我们来个回锅肉。”

“回锅肉？”服务员拿着点菜机的手停滞了：“我们家菜单上好像没有。”

“没有不可以叫厨师烧一个么，这么简单的家常菜。”

服务员有些为难：“我去问问后厨，应该可以的。”

“不是说点素的？”莫小煊问，“回锅肉是素的？”

“是啊，里面有菜的都算素的，再说你看一盘回锅肉里也没几块肉。”

一个嫌弃的表情浮现在了服务员的脸上，莫小煊也觉得有些丢人，秦朗说话有些颠三倒四，还总想揩餐厅油水，可是微信了解到他的家庭条件不差啊，难道他是想试探我？

“我看够了吧。”莫小煊提议，“就这些吧。”

“汤还没点呢！”秦朗宠溺地看了她一眼，“你们女孩子要多喝汤。”

莫小煊看着图片上五颜六色的汤，这家餐厅的汤非常有特色，不同的汤搭配了不同颜色和形状的餐具，看起来更加地诱人。

“这个吧，小吊梨汤。”莫小煊指着那道最便宜的汤说。

“小吊梨汤是我们家的特色，”服务员微笑地看着莫小煊，“我们家的小吊梨汤小火慢炖，丝绒般的口感，甘甜清香，每天都有很多回头客。”

“那就这个，价格也很实惠。”莫小煊朝服务员露出一个礼貌的微笑。

“有这样好吗，”秦朗又皱起了眉头，“一壶梨汤就要 38 元，”他惊讶地提高了嗓门儿问服务员：“你知不知道现在菜市场的梨多少钱一斤？”

莫小煊的笑容已经尴尬到凝固，服务员也不再说话。

“主要不是便宜的问题，宝宝，这个价格实在是不公平，我非常生气，”秦朗又转向服务员，“我看你们家不是有那个赠汤，海带鸡蛋汤，也很有营养。”

“那个要满 288 元才有。”

“你先给我们来一份，我们还没点完呢，再说了，以后我们也是回头客，难道不值得你们赠一回汤？”

“好吧，先生，我去给您申请下。”

秦朗满意地点点头，精明的眼珠子在眼眶里打转，他用手摩挲着下巴，看着莫小煊的脸露出了笑容。

“宝贝你再看看有什么想吃的，不要被这些服务员骗了，我啊，最懂他们那点小心思了。”

“够了，够了。”莫小煊将头转向窗外去欣赏风景，努力压住心底的不快。

“怎么可以，我们第一次出来吃饭，你这样让人家看了，觉得我小气。”

服务员在一旁白眼儿要翻上房顶，莫小煊嘴角扯过一丝苦笑。

“我们来个甜品吧。”秦朗指着图片上最便宜的巧克力大白，丝滑地巧克力豆安静地躺在白色的奶油雪糕上，看着图片似乎都飘出了奶香：“这个是什么？”

“巧克力大白，先生。”服务员依旧耐心地微笑。

“我还不知道名字？”秦朗也翻了个白眼：“我问你原材料。”

“原材料这个我也不是很清楚。”

“不是很清楚，那么我来告诉你，这个就是麦丽素加光明奶砖，你这三颗麦丽素就几毛钱，奶砖不超过 5 块钱，你这上面就 28，打劫啊！要不要这样。”

服务员微笑又沉默地望着他，莫小煊觉得有些冷，不知是不是空调开太足的原因，原本的闷热被驱散地一干二净。

“算了，不点了吧。”莫小煊的脸上已经没有了笑容，如果真的是考验，那这也有点过分了，会不会他的家庭条件没那么好，而他一直在骗我。

“不行，怎么能没有甜品，你们女孩子饭后就要来点甜的。”

“你很了解嘛。”莫小煊幽幽地来了句。

秦朗似乎意识到说多了，尴尬地笑了下：“哪有，没见过猪……”

“行了，别说了，没关系，我都可以的。”

“宝宝你真懂事，要不这样吧，我们先在这里吃主食，一会儿我带你去隔壁吃甜品，你们女孩子啊，胃就一点点，不然一会儿吃不下了。”

“你可真细心。”莫小煊眉眼在笑，嘴上已经露出鄙夷，她已经听了 5 遍你们女孩子。

“是吧，你喜欢就好。好了，就这些。”秦朗将菜单递给服务员，服务员机械地抱着点菜机重新报了一遍菜名。

“我们没点米饭。”秦朗补充到。

“米饭是送的，”服务员说：“您需要加随时和我们说。”

“送的！那给我们来一盆。”

莫小煊感觉自己要昏过去了，她好想赶紧离开现场，可是这不是相亲啊，他已经是她的老公了。她开始苦笑了起来，秦朗以为她很开心，更加来劲，冲着服务员吼道。

“怎么啦，客人喜欢你家米饭还不高兴，快去安排。”

服务员走了，莫小煊觉得没话可说了，两人有一腔没一腔地搭茬。菜上好了，秦朗殷勤地给莫小煊夹这夹那。两人吃好后，秦朗看着菜单，又皱起了眉头。

“这个价格……”

“我付好了。”莫小煊收起手机。

“啊！你怎么付的？”

“扫桌面上的二维码。”

“你怎么这样速度啦，今天我们第一次见面吃饭就要你请客，这怎么像样子。”

“没关系，一家人不分这些。”

总归以后要一起生活的，反正秦朗家有房，越是有钱人就越是抠门儿，说不定是在试探自己呢，莫小煊想着。

“你可真懂事，”秦朗说，“那早知道我们就点那个大白，还有什么鱼，宝宝你真能赚钱。”

两个人从餐厅出来，莫小煊准备打车回家。

“别，宝贝你忘了甜品啦，这回一定要我来。”

“哦，隔壁的甜品，走吧。”

莫小煊心想他还是知道这些的，果然他在试探我，我就说他不会那么抠门儿的。一回头，在餐厅隔壁矗立着一家全家便利店，她觉得太阳明晃晃地，爱情似乎被晒死了。

4. 同居生活

“所以你真的决定要离婚？就只是因为他小气吗？”

“你以为只是一般的小气吗？我让你见识见识啥是真正的奇葩。”莫小煊继续和我描述她老公的异常行为。

秦朗有个特殊的爱好——捡垃圾。尽管他家庭条件确实不错，母亲是大学教授，父亲是商人，莫小煊所说的“条件好”，都是真实的，可他真的是热爱捡垃圾。

秦朗的家里随处可见他捡来的“垃圾”，她在他的家里发现了一堆空的矿泉水瓶，破旧的纸箱，以及一小坨一小坨的纸巾，他怀疑那是他从餐厅里顺回来的，脑补出秦朗在餐厅鬼鬼祟祟往口袋里装纸巾的画面，莫小煊觉得又好气又好笑。

莫小煊倒是没亲自看见过他翻垃圾箱，可是有一次，秦朗说他去打篮球，莫小煊想着去看看他吧，给他送瓶水，她的青春还从来没有给在篮球场上的男孩子送过水，想到这她便甜丝丝地带着少女般地殷切赶去篮球场看望他。篮球场的外面，莫小煊老远的就看到了秦朗，他并没有在打球，而是摇摇晃晃地东张西望，手里还拎着什么，是什么呢？莫小煊非常好奇，于是擦了擦眼睛仔细地分辨，她眯起眼睛，努力地聚焦，随着她离秦朗越来越近，她看清楚了，竟然是一个铁锅，她感到难以置信，但随着她越走越近了，她断定秦朗手里拿着的就是一个铁锅，他没有发现她的到来，仍然在铁丝网的篮球场外面像二愣子一样地拿着铁锅摇摇晃晃，仿佛那铁锅就是伴他闯荡江湖的宝剑利器，他一边晃动手里的铁锅一边左顾右盼地认真地寻觅着什么，像个既严肃又漫无目的拾荒者，猛然间看到莫小煊过来了，他身体一僵，眼睛里写满意外，有些紧张地将锅往身后一藏。

“你，你怎么来了？”他一紧张就会结巴。

“这锅哪来的？”莫小煊看着那个缺了牙有些斑驳的铁锅。

“啊？”他没有说是捡来的，支支吾吾解释半天也没说清楚。

那一刻，莫小煊心头涌起莫名地一片凉：这就是我嫁的男人么？她觉得眼前被一片绝望的海水覆盖了。

“只要对你不小气，就不要这么快离婚吧，毕竟……”我说。

“对我那不是一般地小气。”

在买菜做饭这个问题上，秦朗一定要坚持一个买菜另一个做饭的公平原则。有一次莫小煊在餐厅吃完饭，刚好秦朗过来接她，于是莫小煊，对着自己的亲老公说了一句：“你去买单。”结果秦朗一愣，音调提高了八度。

“凭什么我去买单！”

他站了起来，脸因为生气而涨得通红，整个餐厅的人都在看着他们，莫小煊觉得羞耻到了极点。可是莫小煊还是忍下了愤怒和委屈，默默走到前台自己把单给买了。

“没错，我非常确定，一分一秒都过不下去了。”电话另一头的她就要尖叫起来了：“你不知道她还有更过分的。”

他们相约一起删除了所有社交软件以及相亲账号，可是2周后，莫小煊检查秦朗的手机时发现，他的账号完好无损的还在登录，并且，有超过20个女孩子给他留言，翻手机通讯录时，发现有很多奇奇怪怪的名字，充满污言秽语的昵称，有一天莫小煊好奇打过去，对方果然是个女生，并抱怨秦朗以后不要再打电话过来骚扰她了。得知这一切后的莫小煊当然就是吵架，她是个眼睛里容不得沙子的人，可是秦朗的性格也极其易怒，莫小煊吵，他也理直气壮地不肯让步，说那些女生都是朋友。**对待装睡的人，莫小煊不仅想叫醒他，甚至想说教感化他，女人堕入深渊的第一步就是从想拯救一个男人开始，当圣母似乎是每个女人刻在骨子里的天性。**可秦朗拒不承认，莫小煊闹得凶了，他就开始动手，有一次他甚至拿着刀背抵在莫小煊的脖子上，莫小煊瞬间被吓傻了，事后秦朗还嬉皮笑脸地为自己开解，说自己用的是刀背，而不是刀刃，这足以说明他很爱她。

“还有更过分的。”她继续说，此时我们已经保持通话 2 个小时了。

有一次莫小煊的一位小姐妹从北京到厦门去看她，莫小煊就留姐妹在家里留宿，白天莫小煊出门上班，只剩闺蜜和没有工作的秦朗在家。闺蜜在房间里吃水果，只听当当当地敲门声，开门是秦朗，他拨开闺蜜，径直走到床边，躺了下来，说要在这里休息，闺蜜气得拎起包就离开了小煊家。

他极其爱撒谎，并且骗术不高。有一次莫小煊怀疑他的学历造假，他急坏了，尖声尖气地高声叫嚷着说：“我发誓我不是三明学院（一个高职学院）毕业的。”此地无银，他竟然自己说出了真正毕业的院校。

从那以后莫小煊更加坚定了离婚的想法。说到这里对面的莫小煊哭了，我也已经听不下去了，一开始还想劝她隐忍，现在已经恨不得亲自带她去离婚了，哭了不到三分钟。

“但我也很能理解他。”莫小煊突然话锋一转：“你知道吗？其实他挺可怜的。”

天！我就知道她要说这个，**这么多年我听了无数姐妹吐槽，吐到最后无不是一句：他很可怜。接下来就是原谅，反反复复，永无止境地循环。他的可怜和我有什么关系呢，难道全天下的穷人都是我的穷人？全天下的可怜人都可以因为一份可怜而抹去所有罪过，那么要监狱干什么呢？**我已经预感到接下来她要说啥了，但是流程还是要走，于是我又开始倾听可恨之人必有可怜之处的那一份可怜。

他有重度抑郁症和轻度精神病，很小的梗他能哈哈哈大笑个半天，并且笑声类似于尖叫，接近咆哮，稍经训练就是海豚音，那尖叫让人怀疑他似乎从来没有笑过。或者瞬间生气，嘴角带着眼皮连着眼角纹儿一起走向地心，然后对着墙壁大骂特骂，你觉得他情绪燃到极点的时候，又瞬间露出笑脸，这瞬间的切换让观者头皮发麻，自己也要被引入躁怒不安的情绪黑洞。

于是莫小煊好好地分析了他的原生家庭，这半年来，她已经成了半个心理专家了。

他父母在他小时候就开始做生意，经常把他一个人锁在家里，孤独和自闭导致了他耽于幻想，失去了和人正常交往的能力，并且极其没有安全感。小的时候，他总是一个人眼巴巴地望着窗外，从早晨等到晚上，终于等到了爸妈的身影，父母带着一身的风尘仆仆回到家，见到家里一片狼藉便开始数落他，忙碌了一天的大人，已经耗尽了耐心，于是毫无顾忌地将情绪丢给秦朗，小小的他眼里噙着泪花不敢反驳，他怕自己一旦发怒，父母就不要他了，他们经常说这样的话不是么。可是当有一天他意识到，父母的那些话不过是唬孩子的，便放肆地开始了无所顾忌的人生，他需要父母，也痛恨父母。经常唆使莫小煊一起不要相信父母，有一次秦朗母亲叫莫小煊发身份证件照过去办理一些手续。

“不要发给她，”秦朗尖声尖气地叫着，“万一她拿去做什么坏事怎么办。”

一开始莫小煊觉得秦朗太不是个东西了，可是和他的父母接触久了，就理解了秦朗的怀疑，发现这一家都不是“一般人”啊！

他的父亲和母亲并不住在一起，双方的财务也是各自独立，母亲在大学管理创新创业的项目，经常从学校的各种教育经费里揩油，并且她做这些龌龊之事的经历丝毫不避讳孩子，常常在家里炫耀自己又免费拿了哪几家创业公司的股份，捞到了多少公款。父亲呢，对家里的大事小情不闻不问，对妻子不管不顾，对秦朗就像没这个孩子一般。因此家里就是母亲一手遮天，她的精神思想也直接影响了整个家庭。

“那真是个恐怖的家庭！”莫小煊的声音都有些颤抖：“据说他父亲还爱上了他妈妈的妹妹。”

“谁的妹妹。”我听得头都大了。

“就是秦朗的小姨。他经常和我说自己是他小姨的孩子，不是妈妈亲生的。”

“你带他去过精神病院么？”我觉得这不单单是情绪的问题了。

“去过。”莫小煊说：“但是到了门口我就不忍心了，他跪下来，嚎啕大哭，像孩子一样求我，说去了精神病院我会不会不要他了。”

可秦朗已经不是第一次去精神病院了，他也想积极配合治疗，但没有什么效果。莫小煊的声音开始哽咽，我知道她还是心疼他，**只要一个女人还心疼一个男人，那么无论这个男人犯了多大的错，她都一定会回头。**

我在想在秦朗的世界，又是怎样一片更加绝望的海洋，他看不到自己，不知道自己的灵魂栖居在哪里，甚至即使看到了，也无法将自己打捞出海面，当他碰到了莫小煊，觉得生活有了一丝转机，即便这个人不能带他逃离出自己崩溃的世界，起码可以一起到海中来陪伴他了。**于是在我的想象中，秦朗的面目狰狞了起来，那是一个堕于无奈的、既可怜又可恨的魔鬼。**

当莫小煊提出离婚时，秦朗的母亲自然是不同意，她一直在数落自己的儿子，还当着莫小煊的面扇了秦朗一个耳光，看到这一幕的莫小煊动容了，并且因为母亲真挚的态度而选择了原谅，可是秦朗仍然没有改进，但是莫小煊学会了去秦朗母亲那里告状。

“别跟他一般见识，小煊，”秦朗母亲拉着她的手，笑嘻嘻地看着她，“你不知道我有多喜欢你。”接下来就一番对莫小煊的夸奖和认可。

听到这些的莫小煊再次动容了，她是个耳根子及其软的人。

“实在不行，就咱俩过了，你管他干嘛呢？咱俩以姐妹相处。”秦朗母亲笑着说。

听到这句莫小煊感动的泪水都快掉下来了。

“女人二婚可不好找对象了呀！”母亲带着一脸慈祥继续补刀，“再说你们以后有了孩子啊，我们会好好教育他，我这个婆婆全心思帮你带，小孩肯定错不了。”

莫小煊点点头，觉得也算有了些安慰。

“你看啊，我就这么盘算着，”秦朗母亲一手拉着莫小煊的手，另一只手拍着她的手背，“等将来你有了孩子啊，每个月你出一万块，我出一万块，一个月两万，小孩子的生活费也就够了。还有那房子，我们家那几套呢地理位置都不算好，而且都租出去了，不如我们一起贷款在市中心买个好的，你一个月三四万在这里……”

没等听完，莫小煊就赶紧抽出了手，逃离了现场，回来的路上她眼泪狂涌，自己是掉进了怎样的一个土匪窝啊！

她现在的处境就是没有人帮她，周围人不理解她，新婚共同生活还不到一个月，她马上提出离婚，周围的人都觉得她疯了。并且每次一提出离婚，秦朗就跪下来，眼泪纵横地求她，而且全家恨不得集体给她下跪，这个善良的女孩哪里经得住这样的道德绑架，乖乖地妥协了，这一妥协就是半年，对她来说却像半生那样漫无止尽的黑暗。

这期间莫小煊发现秦朗竟然还有个前妻，经历了各种奇葩待遇的她一开始接收到这个消息并没有很震惊，甚至有一天，在她和秦朗大吵完后，她觉得实在受不了，于是翻出了老早偷着存好的前妻号码打了过去。

“我劝你还是再忍一忍，”前妻在电话另一头带着平稳的语气说，“他这个人啊，是很好哄的，你甭跟他动真感情，他说什么你就听，生气了，你就哄，你看他那精神状态，能活久么？并且啊，你不要看他到处撩女孩子，他那方面不行的。”前妻在电话了发出一声冷笑：“所以说，姐妹我劝你，忍一忍，他死了，财产就都是你的了，不要步我后尘，哎！我当初就是实在没法忍了，出轨了，这不就出局了，但是我看好你，支持你。”

莫小煊的三观崩了。从那以后她决定了，必须离婚，否则自己会被这个家庭吃干抹净。

可是每次她一提离婚，他一祈求，她就心软。最接近离婚的那一次，他们都到了民政局，秦朗一身西装，拿着一束 10 块钱的玫瑰花，又跪了下来，身后是他的父母和母亲的学生，集体求她不要离婚，莫小煊的恻隐之心哪里经得过这样的轰炸，再次缴械投降了。

一个风和日丽的周日下午，莫小煊因为一条贵重的项链找不到了，于是去质问秦朗。

“我没有拿。”秦朗眼珠子在眼眶中打转，目光不敢直视她，莫小煊二话不说便上了楼，翻箱倒柜开始找。

“你在干什么？”秦朗怒吼到。

莫小煊无视这句怒吼，继续翻找项链，她翻箱倒柜都没有找到，打开电脑桌旁的一个抽屉，赫然间无数条项链出现在眼前，里面全部都是珠宝饰品，戒指项链耳环，莫小煊看呆了。

“你哪来这些东西？”莫小煊问。

秦朗猴子一样地蹿到莫小煊面前，合上抽屉：“谁让你翻的！”

“你怎么会有这么多女孩子的饰品？是不是偷的？”

可能是由于听到偷的这两个字，秦朗有些慌了：“我没偷，这些都是我前女友的。”

经过一番盘问，莫小煊终于了解到，原来秦朗不仅对自己抠门儿，就连曾经送前女友的饰品也要在分手后要回来。就连和前妻的结婚戒指，他离婚后都要了回来。

莫小煊实在受不了了，她没有继续找到项链，但是那一刻她崩溃到了极点，所有积压的怒火让她不能控制自己，她打了秦朗两下。然而秦朗竟然也打回了她两下，莫小煊崩溃了，开始嚎啕大哭。秦朗没有哄她，而是毫无耐心地叫她离开这里，她一边哭一边说不走。秦朗就开始拖着她往屋子外面拽，莫小煊不配合，他就死死地拖住她，把她从二楼生生拖到了一楼，又拖到门外，大门一关。莫小煊被拖得遍体鳞伤站在门外哭嚎，可是也没人理会。

从那以后她就经常被家暴。

她就那样待在绝望的坑里，怪大家不去救她，可是要怎么救呢，每次下定决心离开后，由于怜悯，由于道德压力，由于不甘心，她总是自己又走回去。这样反复了几十次，有一次她打给我说真的要离了，已经法律介入并且分居了。

我终于看到了一丝希望。

5. 绝望之路

又过了半年，莫小煊又从厦门来上海玩，我见她精神气色很好，以为她离婚的事情已经处理干净了。

“还没呢，还在耗着。”说这话时，她脸上看不出多少的悲伤，我想她可能已经有些麻木了。

“啊！是他纠缠你还是怎么？”

然后她又开始讲起了她这长达半年来的离婚路程。

“我就是要耗着她。”这是秦朗和律师表达的态度，得不到的将其悔之，他耗了前妻 2 年才同意离婚，至于在莫小煊身上要耗多久，全看他心情。莫小煊去法院申诉这种不公，可是法律并没有对莫小煊有什么保护，更恐怖的是，秦朗的母亲又是法律学教授，妥妥一个有文化的流氓家族，莫小煊连缴械投降的资格都被剥夺了。

那段时间，莫小煊差点得了抑郁症，法律上莫小煊不仅一分钱分不到，（可是莫小煊已经不在乎这些了，她只想尽快逃离，）而且只要秦朗不签字，离婚协议书就无法生效。于是莫小煊到处打听求人，请律师，无助卑微到了尘埃里，这个社会，喜欢雪中送炭的人少之又少，大多数人喜欢锦上添花，还有一些人喜欢火上浇油，莫小煊的婚姻已经很不堪了，可是周围的同情并没有多，突然间出现了很多经验颇丰的“指路人”。有的人要把她介绍给有权有势的本地人，这样莫小煊就有了依靠，莫小煊去见过那个“本地人”，又老又猥琐，她觉得这更像是一种献祭，自己从一个火坑跳向另一个火坑罢了，于是莫小煊委婉地拒绝了。

她还有一个搞艺术的朋友，思想很是开放，于是她开始给莫小煊洗脑，说莫小煊的一切还和没结婚的时候一样，无非就是多了一张结婚证，她开车带莫小煊去民政局领张离婚证就完事了，一切还和以前一样。于是莫小煊信以为真了，每天跟着搞艺术的朋友去酒吧喝酒，一开始莫小煊很中意这样的麻醉，可后来就发现自己的状态越来越糟糕，情绪越来越崩溃。我劝莫小煊没事去跑跑步，多思考，还给她寄了运动手环，可她不想运动，她更愿意安静地一个人待在绝望悲伤情绪中，觉得那样比较安全；有人劝她去读书，她说自己看不下去；有人劝她和家人商量，她觉得给家里丢人，即便后悔死了，可是到现在她都没有和自己家里人说过自己结婚的事情，觉得自己太丢人了，不想让家人和自己一样承担压力，所以这所有的一切她打算自己解决后再汇报家里。

她不是懦弱，只是在痛苦中无力自拔了。这段时间秦朗也没消停，她一边继续撩着新的妹子，另一头还给莫小煊发挽回的消息，她的恻隐之心慢慢变得麻木，最终只想离婚，而他的一切行为（那只病态的变色龙，时而跪下来恳求她，时而魔鬼一般地殴打她，时而又像孩子一样对莫小煊有依赖），在她眼里，全是戏。

可我突然发现这个社会，强者往往是善于剥夺的侵略者，并且他们极其善于伪装，扮作人畜无害，家事教养良好的样子，吸引来猎物便将其生吞活剥，都说这社会进化了，可它从古至今都是丛林法则，只是玩家换了一批又一批，包装成了不同的外壳。

在好心律师的帮助下，一年后她终于从婚姻中解脱出来。这一年秦朗始终骚扰她，她也一直忍住了没再回去。

离完婚的那一天，秦朗扒着出租车的大门，跪在地上哭着恳求她，那一天是平安夜。

“我给你买苹果还不行么？”他孩子一样求她，仿佛苹果是个天大的礼物。

“你有病！”

莫小煊用尽全身力气，一脚踹开扒着车门的秦朗，这一年的无奈，隐忍，痛恨，同情，绝望，希望，爱恨交织的矛盾挣扎，汲汲不得的幻想现实，都伴随着那狠狠地一脚，像秦朗一样，箭一般地飞了出去，“咣”的一声车门关闭，莫小煊扬长而去，坐在出租车里，她想起结婚那一天，她娇羞地和他坐在出租车上，而今天竟然一脚踹开了自己的前夫，她突然间觉得很好笑，笑着笑着鼻子就酸了。

去年此地，只见新人笑；

今时此刻，却笑旧人哭。

人世间的苍凉在她眼前形成了一道透明的屏障，一触碰便化为了水蒸气，随之而来的是汩汩的泪水，她终于学会了对乞求冷漠，她终于变得坚定而强大。

“你这小丫头，心可真狠啊！”多事的司机愤愤不平：“男孩子都那么可怜了，给他一次机会吧。”

“闭嘴！开你的车！”莫小煊朝司机大吼了一声，眼泪却决堤了。

可怜和可恨不会相互抵消，就像功劳和过错无法相互抵消，他们只是相互掩埋，平行存在，你方去罢我登场，作为社会人，总要承受矛盾。

平安夜 party 上，一堆朋友正在等待着莫小煊，恭喜她逃出魔掌。可是这魔掌到底是谁的，是秦朗家庭，还是她自己的内心，还是这阴霾天空下对女性群体的无形之网，莫小煊不得而知。

她庆幸自己终是逃脱了！

6. 希望之光

在经历了 3 天的恋爱扯证，3 年的撕扯离婚后，她再一次恢复单身，可她还不到 30 岁，在婚姻市场上的价值直接打了 5 折，离过婚的女人总是莫名其妙地被人诟病，不好嫁。离婚后的莫小煊再次去相亲真实地体会到了二婚女性的痛。正当年的年轻男孩，上来先看她条件，这回不是她看别人的条件了，房子，工作，工资，全盘核问，最后一听二婚，立马买单走人。

她的一个老师朋友，建议她赶紧找下一个男人，有了靠山就可以对付秦朗，不然她一个人孤立无援，万一秦朗什么时候再找上来不好处理。于是那位朋友介绍了莫小煊一个建设局的局长给莫小煊，她看着即将迈入老年的建设局局长，饭都没吃完就回来了。

“怎么你还嫌弃，”老师朋友感到不可思议，“你都是二婚女人了，婚恋市场上能找到这样的也不错了，人家局长可是从来没结过婚。”老师朋友眼神一挑，嘴一撇：“况且，人家那工作油水多，不知道多少姑娘奔着。”言外之意，莫小煊这个二婚一地鸡毛的女人要识相，认命，命运就不会亏待你。

可是在莫小煊的眼里，自己根本就没有享受过婚姻生活，这太不公平了，在莫小煊的眼里，自己和没结婚没区别，可法律上，自己怎么就成已婚人士了，她觉得一肚子委屈。

她去学校教课，觉得所有人都在背后议论自己，走在路上，也觉得抬不起头来，那段时间她又快得了抑郁症。她在心里抗拒自己离异，如果时间可以回到那个下午多好，她一定不会和那个人进民政局，她从未想过，一段冲动的婚姻会给她带来巨大的压力和心态巨大的改变，年纪轻轻的她已经少了许多活力和热情，看起来像暮气沉沉的夕阳。可是每天又要把自己收拾得精精神神的，因为周围一堆人等着看她的笑话，她去学校里，同事都对她笑，可是眼神却像是嘲笑，有的嘴里还啧啧地发出同情可怜的声音来，她装作没看见，可是每经历一次这样的场景，她的心就划过一道伤痕。

于是在狐朋狗友的撺掇下，她又开始不停地去相亲。

现代年轻人有一种虚空的乐观，仿佛肆无忌惮地向前走就是一种力量，就可以抹去曾经的狼藉满地，可那只是对过往不堪以及现实的一种逃避。

莫小煊好歹是新时代的独立女性，工作好，有钱有颜，可是厦门人不在乎那，你离婚了，没本地户口，就什么都不行。我常常惊异于某些发达地区人类的思维，你看那城市，高楼林立，灯火繁华，人们光鲜亮丽，出入各种剧院商场，可是思维还保留在 100 年前，无法欣赏跳脱于传统的任何美和冒险精神。

到底是物质发展太快，还是精神发展太慢，我已经无法区分了。

甚至连我的朋友们也是这个样子，叫我不要与莫小煊往来，怕我被带坏了。我对母亲的态度不置可否，可这些冷漠深深触痛了我，难道这世间见到弱者就都想着赶紧逃离，免得沾了一身晦气吗？可如果有一天我成了弱者，或者现在我就是弱者，也或许正在读我文字的读者是个弱者，我们又要逃向何方。茫茫人海，人们的冷漠势力所铸成的围墙，将所有善良信仰丢失在九霄云外。强者跋扈，弱者相欺，这是人间。

“我买房子了。”

距离她离婚后的又一个整年后，我再次接到了她的电话。

我不知道她怎样熬过了这一整年，我经常见她发到处吃喝玩乐的朋友圈，用她的话来说，太多的人等着看她的笑话了，不能让他们得逞。她就是深夜里哭死，第二天还是要戴上阳光明媚的面具。她狂吃，胖了就去抽脂，尽管方法极端，可她还是在努力地维持尊严，一个人只要懂得维护尊严，就不会垮塌，尽管方法愚钝，濒临死地，可是熬过那一个个绝望的夜晚，她竟然奇迹般地复生了。

“我以前就是太缺爱了，太需要男人陪了，所以总是心软。”

有一天小煊回老家，在客厅里弹钢琴，琴声悠扬，莫小煊长长的头发垂落下来，看起来忧郁又动人，母亲在一旁看着她，泪眼婆娑了，突然上前抱住她。

“煊，妈知道你的事了。”于是母亲抱着她哭了起来，莫小煊吓到了，听到母亲的哭声，她没有抬头，将头深深地埋在母亲的胸前，眼泪无声地浸透了母亲的衣衫。她从小到大被家里人悉心培养，期待走向一个光明的未来，可是这充满心血的培养，并没有为她的婚姻幸福带来夹持，大概女性的优秀在婚姻的规则里本身就是个悖论，以为是幸福的加分项，实际是婚姻的献祭品。莫小煊哪里会总结这些，她也开始嚎啕大哭，母女两个人依偎在一起，这段婚姻对这个普通家庭造成的伤害，太深了。

于是家里人出了首付，帮她在厦门买了房，现在她只需要每个月还贷款。

以前她总是找那些条件好，有很多房子的男人，而现在她想拥有一所属于自己的房子，在失去了许多人生中的宝贵东西后，她决定自己抓住幸福：不管是物质的，还是精神上的，她希望那份幸福来自自己，而不是别人。她努力地希望通过一束光，将更多的阳光洒满生活，让狼藉的过去重新焕发生机。

“即便这辈子我莫小煊嫁不出去了，我也不怵了。”

可此刻我觉得她在闪闪发光。我的朋友莫小煊，她不是个高智商的人，耿直地活，并且用力过猛，可她无法忍受无趣的人生。她从风雨中来，又在苦海中渡，最后在血泪中学会：真正的独立是内心的底气，不是外在的所谓“好条件”。

又过了一年，莫小煊去俄罗斯拿到了钢琴博士，归国便达到了年薪百万，她不仅摆脱了那个男人给他造成的伤害，还将社会对她的偏见一一击回，从一片狼藉废墟中建起了金光闪闪的事业大厦。

将一个女人的成就和婚姻来挂钩，实在是太不公平了！太不公平了！

一个女人婚姻成功，没错，这算成就，可是婚姻不成功，也不该归为人生失败。就像这社会不会因为一个男人的一次创业失败就否定他今后的人生吗，女性的婚姻失败也不该被全盘否定。太阳东升西落，光辉公平地洒在每一个人的身上，再荒凉的地带都有顽强的生命在涌动，每个生命都应该有重新来过的机会。

我认为我的这篇文章不仅仅写给女性，更是写给千千万万个历经风雨的平凡普通人，一个人无法选择出生，但可以选择生活。我真心地希望自己以及我的读者都能有莫小煊一样彪悍面对人生的勇气。

莫小煊，她终究成就了自己。她自己就是英雄。

Miss/Mrs Mo

People must often confront darkness,

or they will fail to learn to capture light

1.The Girl Who Yearns to Marry

Mo Xiaoxuan was my high school classmate. we didn′t have much interaction during high school but we have been in touch for many years from college to work. Although we chatted haphazardly, we have become one of the longest-running companions of each other. While we can′t be called soulmate, we can still be considered people with whom we can share our thoughts and concerns.

We have completely different personalities. I was somewhat introverted, enjoying quiet moments alone. She was naturally lively and animated. When she laughed, she gave a broad grin with a loud and expansive voice. Despite that, she was exceptionally beautiful, with grape-like big eyes, a nose that was as straight and perfect as a model from a plastic surgery clinic, a well-proportioned figure, and fair skin like almond tofu. There was always a touch of innocence and romanticism in her gaze, and joy seemed to effortlessly radiate from her eyes, making her mischievous and adorable. She rarely concealed her emotions and had clear likes and dislikes. If you didn′t like her, you wouldn′t be able to continue a conversation after just three sentences. However, once you were attracted to her personality, it would lead to a solid and genuine friendship.

Her sense of righteousness was filled with firepower. She was willing to seek through Xiamen just to get you the potato ice cream you loved. If anyone dared to bully you, she would be the first to step up and fight for justice on your behalf. Sitting in home, you would receive specialty products mailed to you from various parts of the world. She was carefree and hot-tempered, but once she liked you, she would unleash all her patience and happily engage in various activities you liked just to please you. Despite being less reserved, who could resist her warm-hearted gestures?

The last time I saw her was at an Italian restaurant full of plants. The restaurant was very spacious, with many tropical flowers and plants indoors, along with a serene little pond. We seated by the pond, near a large hanging orchid. The atmosphere was incredibly refreshing. Normally, she would be busy immersing herself in such an environment, taking pictures, and enjoying herself. However, she had a gloomy expression on her face today. She had been gently stroking the hanging orchid for the past ten minutes, and her eyelashes, like brushes, drooped down. It seemed as though even the neighboring plants could sense the melancholic aura of a disappointed girl. The dishes arrived; she ordered a salad while I chose a pizza, along with some pasta and snacks.

“What′s the matter?”

“I want to lose weight.” she forcefully poked at

the pizza as if it was her enemy.

"That's it?"

She looked at me, her eyes becoming speechless, and silently sighed.

"Don't you feel anxious?" She asked.

"Anxious about what?"

"Getting married! We're not getting any younger."

So, that was the reason. My heart relaxed a bit.

"Why are you so anxious?"

"Can I take it easy? We're almost 30. Regardless of pressures from all directions, Difficulty in childbirth will also become a problem."

I had already eaten almost half of my pizza while she was still poking at the vegetables on the other side, but at least she had stopped bothering the hanging orchid.

"Then tell me, what's your plan? What should we do?" I pushed the snacks toward her.

She pursed her lips, her big eyes still carrying

mischief and cuteness, but not as fearless as before.

"Let me tell you, I′ve been on blind dates for almost a year. I am a regular customer of various dating apps, online dating sites, and matchmaking co rners."

"Activist," I commented, twirling the pasta on my plate, "So why do you still look like this? Keep going on blind dates until you find the Mr. Right."

"Ouch! razzle-dazzle blind dates."

"What happened?"

"All sorts of weirdos are there!"

She began to ramble, telling me about the bizarre encounters she had on dating wcbsites. Such as the "Dumas" who drove recklessly fast, a revolutionary youth of the 1970s who called her comrade Mo every day on WeChat, and an experienced scumbag who dated her and her best friend in the same haft a month.

"What should I do? I′m exhausted," she finally picked up a slice of pizza and started indulging in human food.

"Maybe you should try introductions from people around you instead. Online platforms are unreliable."

"Those are poor quality." She was a piano teacher with a studio in Xiamen. "Maybe you can introduce me to some Mr. Perfects in your circle."

I glanced at her while continuing to eat the pasta in front of me. She had mentioned this before over the years. It′s not that I didn′t want to introduce her to someone, but the truth was she didn′t fit the criteria. The aesthetic standards for handsome and wealthy guys were quite uniform, and Wang Sicong led the aesthetic vision of 98% of Chinese men. Leaving that aside, their requirements for personality were also quite uniform: gentle, submissive, and less self-oriented, someone who appeared easier to control. Apparently, Mo Xiaoxuan didn′t fit into any of these categories. Although she was beautiful, she didn′t have the looks of an internet celebrity, and her personality was too vibrant.

"I'll introduce another time." I placated her with a vague response.

On that day, she kept asking me for advice, but I didn't have a better solution. I wasn't interested in blind dates and was fully focused on my work. It seemed that at our age, and even a few years younger, many women were eager to get married quickly. However, the reason why these women couldn't find a suitable partner was not because there were no pursuers; rather, most men did not meet their standards. The men who did meet their standards often had numerous other women, even goddess-like figures, around them. Moreover, nowadays, many young men are incredibly proud, regardless of whether their own conditions are good or not. They put a lot of effort into their appearance, from makeup to plastic surgery, while not necessarily striving for success in their careers or in pursuing women. In their hearts, they probably want to find a beautiful and rich woman. Thus, the standards for choosing a partner in this era have become highly focused on appearance.

We went back home after that gathering. She lived in Xiamen and worked as a piano teacher at a university. Meanwhile, she also ran two piano studios. She was excellent, but that didn't really matter. **In this society, people won't praise a woman for her excellence, instead, they would criticize her if she hasn't been married off.** Mo Xiaoxuan's sense of inferiority stemmed from this. She may not really like handsome and wealthy men, nor did she necessarily need someone else's money. It's just that handsome and wealthy men are the "good standards" set by society, and who doesn't have a bit of vanity? In my view, Mo Xiaoxuan wasn't lacking in money, and she was willing to spend on others. She always stood up for what was right. However, if she were to be expected to buy a house or a car, it would indeed be a bit unfair to her.

I had been preparing for the GMAT exam for

half a year, but my scores were always disappointing. I wasn't in a hurry to get married like Mo Xiaoxuan, and perhaps that was the reason. It's not that I considered myself exceptionally independent or lofty, but I often felt a sense of liberation when I immersed myself in work. What was this sense of liberation? It was the liberation from the societal pressures and formulaic expectations of getting married, having children, and following a predetermined path in life. I had been bombarded with these questions since my university days, and they continued to linger even now. However, I always believed that I could do something more. Yet, I also frequently doubted myself. Although I worked to earn money for myself, more often than not, the money ended up being earned by others. If I got married, I would become someone else's wife. I may give birth to my kids, but in the end, they would belong to someone else's family. Even I would belong to someone else's family. **If defining a woman's value by marriage,**

then from birth to death, she would never truly belong to herself. Everything she does would be attributed to love and be dedicated to others, leaving behind, at most, a monument of motherhood. But most women don′t even have that monument. After their youth, mental prowess, and reproductive abilities are depleted, they are often prematurely sidelined. Sometimes you feel like society has progressed, but this progress only makes the weak more embarrassed and the strong prouder.

One day, I was reviewing for the GMAT. The grammar drove me nuts. I was a person who was good at application but poor at theory. Hence, when I climbed the peak of grammar, I was stranded at the foot of the mountain even if my oral English was very excellent. Just as I was furrowing my brows and having a headache, Mo Xiaoxuan called me. The moment I answered the phone, I felt a sense of relief, knowing that I could have a relaxing chat with her. However, on the other end, I heard Mo Xiaoxuan′s excited scream, nearly causing me to throw my phone away. What followed was her voice trembling with excitement.

"I′m telling you," she rarely called my name, in her address, I was simply "you", "I got married!"

This time, it was my turn to scream.

"What?! Weren′t you just here with me less than a month ago?"

"Yes, I got married."

I didn′t want to hear her repeat. I was impatient and eager to hear the whole story from start to finish. So, under my insistence, she began to recount the entire process of her whirlwind marriage.

2.The First Met

She stood in front of the Civil Affairs Bureau wearing a white shirt, her hands tightly gripping the thin strap of her LV bag, palms starting to sweat. The weather wasn′t particularly sunny; it was rather dull as if a layer of gauze had draped over everything. Mo Xiaoxuan′s grape-like big eyes were locked firmly in the direction from which the car would come. Her long eyelashes covered nearly one-sixth of her face. Sweat beads formed on her fair forehead and perfectly sculpted, high-bridged nose, while anxiety and unease in her gaze seemed to dim the weather even further. She glanced at the time on her phone, pursed her peach-colored lips, and turned around, pacing back and forth at the entrance.

"It′s only been three days!" Her anxiety

accelerated her heartbeat. She had known him for just three days, and they had met on a social networking app.

The only love experience of Mo Xiaoxuan ended in a short period of time with failure. She was already 28 years old this year. Reluctantly, she embarked on the path of blind dates. **For a woman approaching 30 years old, her attitude towards marriage was like catching the last bus late at night. If she didn′t desperately chase after it, she would miss it.** She frequently browsed various blind date websites and social networking apps, enduring half a year of introductions from parents, relatives, and friends. She had also experienced various methods employed by self-proclaimed "matchmaking gods."

She is naturally fond of laughter and enjoys it. Although she appeared outgoing, she was also easily hurt. As an unmarried woman with attractive facial features, finding a morally upright young man of suitable age was as difficult as finding a swan among a flock of ducks. After all, the story of the Ugly Duckling turning into a beautiful swan only existed in fairy tales. After encountering people from almost all 12 zodiac signs and 56 ethnic groups, she grew weary. She was tired of being treated like a commodity, matched and labeled as if she were a product on a shelf. If she continued down this path, even her moral values would crumble. Thus, she retreated into her shell like a snail. But everything changed when she met Qin Lang three days ago.

At first, she casually matched with a boy whose profile picture was refreshing and clean. He spoke gently and politely, paying great attention to details. He would carefully read every message she sent and respond at the appropriate time. It was precisely because of this that within the first three minutes, he gained Mo Xiaoxuan′s favor. Ten minutes later, a small flame ignited in Mo Xiaoxuan′s heart. She caught a glimpse of hope and gradually reached out, wanting to take another step forward.

Through chatting, she learned that Qin Lang's family owned four properties in Xiamen. His father was in business, and his mother was a university professor. Such a good family background also left a good impression on her.

"Don't miss him!" she contemplated to herself. As they continued to chat, they grew more compatible. Qin Lang was gentle, considerable, and patient. Every word he wrote showed his meticulous concern for Mo Xiaoxuan.

After chatting for a while, she felt herself falling for him. A smile unconsciously appeared on her lips. Shc hardly slept a wink that night. They talked until 4 a.m. She managed to sleep for four hours, then went to teach a piano class to her students. During class, her thoughts kept drifting back to her conversations with Qin Lang. A smile spread across her face unconsciously. For the first time. she felt that the class lasted an eternity. Even when she quickly checked her WeChat messages in the restroom, she couldn′t help but smile. Her heart was no longer under her control.

The next day, still on the chat app, the two of them began discussing their family backgrounds, past relationships, and every detail, no matter how trivial.

"What a considerate and attentive boy!"

Mo Xiaoxuan thought to herself. He cared about every detail of her past, even affectionately calling her "baby" and assuring her that difficulties would pass. He was willing to cherish her. In the eyes of Mo Xiaoxuan, who was struggling alone in the city, this was a gentle bomb that exploded on her emotionally barren land, creating a mushroom cloud of love. Accompanied by tears of emotion, that gentle profile picture on the screen held extraordinary significance in her heart.

On the third day, Mo Xiaoxuan was in a state of excitement, feeling that everything in life had become gentle. Whether it was a living or a dead thing, parents, students, a water cup, or even inanimate objects were filled with tenderness in her eyes. Her life seemed to be a bit disoriented as if she had suddenly fallen from a cold world into a warm spring. Happiness came too suddenly. What surprised her, even more, was that Qin Lang seriously asked her if she wanted to get married.

"Maybe we could get a marriage certificate!"

It was Mo Xiaoxuan who proposed this idea, in the 68th hour, 39 minutes, and 47 seconds since they first met.

"Are you sure?!!! Baby."

Qin Lang replied to message without hesitation.

"So, are you scared? Or you don′t like me?"

She sent an expression with a pouting face. Three minutes passed without a reply from the other side, and Mo Xiaoxuan was on the verge of tears. It was in the third minute and four seconds.

"I can be your husband whenever you want, baby."

The air is humid. A warm mist rose from the

asphalt road after the water truck passed by, making Mo Xiaoxuan feel a warm sensation on her calves. In July, streets in Xiamen were filled with fruit vendors, with colorful and dazzling fruits like summer totems, bustling and vibrant. A blue taxi drove in the distance and slowly stopped in front of Mo Xiaoxuan. She swallowed nervously, her heart racing once again. The car door opened, and a man emerged. After closing the door, he walked up to Mo Xiaoxuan.

"Mo Xiaoxuan?"

The man said with a smile, revealing slightly yellowed teeth. He was also wearing a white shirt and had a pair of gold-rimmed glasses. His round and lively eyes were set in a small face, giving him a somewhat dry appearance. He had a slim figure, and although he seemed a bit tired, he still appeared gentle, clean, and fresh.

"Qin Lang?"

Qin Lang nodded, and a hint of joy appeared in the corner of Mo Xiaoxuan´s eyes. She couldn´t help but giggle, exposing her adorable little tiger teeth. “You look pretty much the same as in the photos. It seems you weren′t deceiving me.”

Qin Lang stared at Mo Xiaoxuan for a few seconds, as if he had fallen into a beautiful vortex before he could react. His eyes seemed to have found a shining pearl.

“You are different from the photo,” Qin Lang lowered his gaze and scratched his head, “You look more beautiful than the photo.”

Mo Xiaoxuan laughed even more joyfully, making a gurgling sound, and her cheeks flushed with crimson: “You′re so sweet-tongued!”

Qin Lang also pulled a smile from the corner of his mouth, his eyes swaying in his eyes, with an expression of excitement, but there was also a hint of strangeness. He eagerly held Mo Xiaoxuan′s hand, never once taking his gaze away from her.

“So, are you satisfied, my girl?”

Mo Xiaoxuan stopped smiling, tears welling

up in her eyes, her heart pounding in her chest. The overwhelming excitement made her overlook any details of observation. She took a deep breath, trying to appear calm.

"Eh," she nodded,"Yes."

"Really?"

Qin Lang's eyes sparkled with delight. It was as if he had just received the emperor's reward or pardon. He tightly held Mo Xiaoxuan's hand and pulled her into his arms. "You are truly beautiful!"

Mo Xiaoxuan's face blushed like a May peony, with bright red in the white. She felt a bit dizzy. "Let's go inside," Qin Lang released Mo Xiaoxuan's shoulder and looked at her face, saying:

"There's still time to regret now." He looked at Mo Xiaoxuan and flashed a mischievous smirk.

"So what!" Mo Xiaoxuan pushed Qin Lang playfully, "Are you regret?"

Without saying a word, Qin Lang grabbed Mo Xiaoxuan's hand and led her into the Civil Affairs

Bureau. Mo Xiaoxuan's heart thumped in her chest as she watched Qin Lang's figure. It all felt somewhat unreal. "I'm getting married!" A mixture of joy, excitement, unease, elation, apprehension, and anticipation flooded her mind, leaving her somewhat numb and unable to think clearly. "I'm almost 30. I can't wait anymore. I have to seize this opportunity and not miss out on a good guy. Why can't we have a flash marriage? It can be romantic too!" Various thoughts, speculations, and fantasies filled her mind, but her steps did not falter for a moment.

With a loud "clang," the seal was placed, and the couple's photos in white shirts looked perfectly matched on the marriage certificate.

"Congratulations!" The civil affairs officer beamed with a smile, extending the congratulations. "Next couple, please!"

Qin Lang held Mo Xiaoxuan's hand, looking at her as if she were a precious treasure. Mo Xiaoxuan felt herself getting lost in his gaze, basking in his love, and experiencing the utmost happiness in life.

"Wifey." he called her, his voice sounding somewhat like a duck, but in the euphoria of the moment, she overlooked such details. His voice was unique and charming in her ears.

"Hubby." she responded, flashing a captivating smile. Mo Xiaoxuan was always smiling, but at this moment, her smile bloomed like a fully opened peony, radiating pure joy.

Qin Lang leaned in and couldn´t help but kiss her on the lips. Mo Xiaoxuan completely lost her ability to think. She felt something in her heart fall into place, a sense of reassurance and security. However, there was also a strange feeling lingering behind, one she couldn´t quite explain. He unabashedly kissed her in the middle of the street, making her feel both shy and excited. She broke free from his embrace.

"There are so many people around!" she pushed Qin Lang lightly.

"Oh!" Qin Lang was slightly disappointed,

but was immediately overshadowed by a joyful expression, "Wifey, where do you want to eat later?"

"Up to you," Mo Xiaoxuan smiled with contentment, her eyes sparkling with happiness and bashfulness. "Hubby!"

The above scenes were all my imagination. I chose this way to present their story fragments to give readers a more vivid experience.

"So, you′re living a happy and snug life just like this?" I looked at the marriage certificate photo sent by Mo Xiaoxuan on the other end of the phone. The date displayed is still yesterday. "It′s too fast. I need some time to catch up."

I admired Mo Xiaoxuan′s executive force. This petite and beautiful girl had such a strong drive. Based on our friendship, I began to admire her even more.

"What′s next?" I asked her.

"What do you mean the next? Of course to live our lives."

"But what about the wedding? Have you bought a house? When are you planning to have a baby?" I regretted asking these questions because I suddenly felt that I seemed very cautious and conservative compared to Mo Xiaoxuan′s carefree attitude. But since I had already asked, there was no going back.

"Let′s take it a step at a time," Mo Xiaoxuan said. "We′re together now, and we′ll overcome all the difficulties that come our way in the future." her voice was full of confidence and hope for the future. I suddenly became excited and started crying.

"Why are you crying?"

"You′re awesome. Happiness really does require proactive pursuit." I felt a surge of warmth covering my heart. Perhaps it was because both Mo Xiaoxuan and I were passionate and sincere people that I always got excited when I heard such passionate and romantic stories.

"Ah, don′t cry anymore. My tears are swirling in my eyes. Just focus on yourself. I′ve already found my happiness."

We talked on the phone for over two hours. After hanging up, it took me a long time to calm my emotions.

What is life? What is marriage? It seems that we are all drawn by an indescribable emotion. Mo Xiaoxuan's marriage seemed a bit hasty to me, but I couldn't help but admire her decisiveness. **Some people always wait for the day when they feel ready to make decisions, and as a result, they procrastinate. But where is that day of readiness? Many things, even if you think about them now, tomorrow, or next year, may still be uncertain. Many opportunities may even be lost due to hesitation. But my friend Mo Xiaoxuan doesn't give hesitation any space to thrive.**

For the challenges encountered in the future life, it's not a big deal to face and take action. Whether this flash marriage will be the balance of happiness or the shackles of marriage, it's hard to say. But she has bravely taken the first step, while I can only pray for her from the other side.

At the same time, my family keeps urging me about getting married. In my mom′s words, "You neither steal the household register nor bring back a boy from outside." Despite inner anxiety, she didn′t recommend I follow Mo Xiaoxuan′s behavior. She was extremely shocked by Mo Xiaoxuan′s situation and warned me that the tough times are yet to come! Because of her attitude, we even had an argument with my complaint that she didn′t understand the thoughts of young people.

"Yes, I don′t understand," she said angrily, "even if you buy a house, it takes a year or two to make a decision. That′s whom you′re going to spend your whole life with!"

"The rich just buy it directly! If they like it, they buy it," I disdainfully dismissed my mom′s thoughts.

"Yeah, you are rich. One day, life will make you cry and howl. And it′s us parents who will foot the bill."

I regarded it as a curse. Just as I was about to argue with her passionately, defending Mo Xiaoxuan and me, she simply closed the door and ignored me.

Sometimes, I also wish I could be like Mo Xiaoxuan, taking a chance and going for a break. What am I afraid of? Even with careful selection, it may not necessarily lead to happiness in the end. Perhaps Mo Xiaoxuan is well versed in this. It's better to settle than to be too picky. Things can be pondered after marriage. The divorce rate is too high in this era. **A decade away, divorces may be commonplace and the marriage may be applauded by others: You are so brave! You're a warrior of this era. Nowadays, marriage should not even be linked to love, and even a stable partnership model may not be guaranteed.**

But I am still full of enthusiasm, hoping to step into marriage. The only question is, where is the destined person? I'm curious, but not in a hurry. Fortunately, I′m always busy, and I have unconsciously forgotten the pressure of these significant life events.

After about a month, I received a phone call.

“What? You′re getting a divorce?”

3.Him

After leaving the Civil Affairs Bureau, Qin Lang hailed a taxi with Mo Xiaoxuan to go to a restaurant. Inside the taxi, Mo Xiaoxuan looked a little nervous and shy as she gazed ahead, seemingly still unable to comprehend the incredibility of just obtaining their marriage certificate. Qin Lang occasionally turned his face to glance at her, his hand instinctively reaching out to hold hers. Mo Xiaoxuan responded by giving his hand a squeeze. Neither of them spoke much. Despite the air conditioning running inside the taxi, the humid summer made Mo Xiaoxuan's forehead slightly perspire.

The taxi stopped by a moderately crowded street, and right in front of them was a restaurant. After Qin Lang paid the fare, they walked towards the restaurant. The interior of the restaurant had a distinct Xishuangbanna style. The black and white patterned floor tiles, the colorful paintings hanging on the clay walls, and the exotic patterns engraved on the tableware all exuded a vibrant and lively atmosphere. The lively and dazzling decorations instantly lifted their mood, and Mo Xiaoxuan began to gradually loosen up.

They chose a relatively quiet place and took their seats. Qin Lang considerately let Mo Xiaoxuan sit on the sofa while he sat on the end of the hardwood chair. The menu was brought over, and the waiter stood nearby, waiting for their selections. Qin Lang gentlemanly handed the menu to Mo Xiaoxuan.

"See what you want."

"I′m fine with anything. It′s up to you."

"Oh, come on. Help yourself," Qin Lang chuckled.

Under this circumstance, Mo Xiaoxuan could refuse anymore, so she scanned the menu carefully.

She had never been to this restaurant before, and the dish names on the menu were quite unique: A Countryside Path (Braised Pig Trotters), Murky Clouds Obscured the Sun (Seaweed and Egg Soup), The Legendary Peppers (Fried Red Pepper with Green Pepper), My Hand Through Your Black Hair (Stewed Pig′s Feet with Kelp).

After watching for a while, Mo Xiaoxuan pointed to a relatively normal dish called Yunnan Grilled Fish.

"This one. Grilled Tilapia," she said, looking at the waiter. " Less chili peppers, please."

"Won′t this make the body get inflamed?" Qin Lang looked at the menu and shook his head. "This kind of grilled fish looks quite big, but it is hard to chew with little meat. There′s not much edible portion. Most of the meat is dry and stuck to the bones. Don′t order it."

"Well, do you have any better suggestions?" Mo Xiaoxuan blinked her grape-like eyes.

"If you want to eat fish, how about this one?" Qin Lang pointed at a picture of Tongue Fish with Tomato Sauce. The bright red soup with white slices of fish looked tender and juicy. "Tongue Fish doesn't have any bones, and it's good for girls to eat more fish!"

Mo Xiaoxuan looked at the price of these two dishes. The latter one is around 20 yuan compared to the former one which was over 80 yuan. She hesitated for a moment, but then quickly dismissed the thought. It shouldn't be about getting something cheaper! The slight dissatisfaction that was about to arise in her heart was immediately quelled.

"Darling, it's okay if you want the Tilapia. I will help you remove the bones so you won't get stuck."

"You're so thoughtful!" Mo Xiaoxuan's momentary doubt was dispelled by Qin Lang's words. "Let's get a Tongue Fish. Removing the bones takes too much time, and both of us won't be able to enjoy our meal that way."

"Wow, you're so sensible."

Mo Xiaoxuan smiled, feeling slightly touched. Qin Lang looked at the menu and pointed to a dish of greens.

"This one, please," he said, pushing up his glasses and glancing at the waiter, then back at Mo Xiaoxuan. "It's good to have a light diet in the hot summer. It's also beneficial for weight loss."

"You're so thin that your soul and body are about to separate!"

"Hey, your girls are the same. Girls always talk about losing weight, even though you're not fat and have a nice and curvy figure."

Mo Xiaoxuan picked up her teacup and took a sip of barley tea, awkwardly swallowing the liquid.

"Xiaoxuan, is there something else you want?"

"Any dish is okay. You can make a decision."

"Come on. Don't be shy. What do you like to eat?"

Mo Xiaoxuan held her teacup, glancing at the

menu in Qin Lang's hand, while the waiter patiently waited by their side.

"How about this one?" Mo Xiaoxuan pointed to the menu where Curry Beef was listed. The beef looked crispy on the outside and tender on the inside, served in a delicate sauce. It was truly mouth-watering. "This looks delicious. It's suitable for weight loss, and I also enjoy eating beef." Mo Xiaoxuan lifted his eyes and looked at Qin Lang.

Qin Lang scratched his head and nodded. "Beef is wonderful, but it seems like measly offerings in the picture, and there are so many potatoes and carrots."

"Excuse me, Sir," the waiter interjected. "There are differences between the physical object and the image."

"I know. The physical object will even be less than the image."

Mo Xiaoxuan frowned and felt even more awkward.

"It's not like this. There might be more. Photos

are mainly for aesthetic…"

"Aesthetic? I′ve been to many restaurants like this. When serving, there are hardly any meat pieces, just vegetables. I even doubt if the meat is real beef." Qin Lang turned his head and looked at Mo Xiaoxuan. "Darling, you have to be careful when eating meat outside. Some unscrupulous restaurants source their meat from somewhere unknown." He glared at the waiter after saying so.

"Sir, you can rest assured that the ingredients are definitely real beef. The meat source is absolutely safe," the waiter reassured with a smile.

"That′s what they all say, but I don′t believe it," Qin Lang persisted. "Xiaoxuan, why don′t you look and choose something else? It′s mainly for your health. When you′re with me in the future, I′ll definitely take good care of your body."

Mo Xiaoxuan blushed. On one hand, she felt even more embarrassed, but on the other hand, she found it somewhat sweet. She took another sip of her tea. "How about this, dear? You decide. I won't be picky."

Qin Lang nodded. "I think it's not good to eat too much meat. Usually, I have a vegetarian diet."

"We also have a variety of vegetarian dishes. Sir, you can flip back."

Qin Lang quickly flipped through the menu and closed it. "Let's have a Twice-cooked Pork."

"Twice-cooked Pork?" The waiter hesitated while holding the ordering device. "It doesn't seem to be on our menu."

"You can ask the cook to make it. Such a simple home-cooked dish."

The waiter looked somewhat embarrassed. "I will wait and ask the cook. It should be no problem."

"Didn't you want something vegetarian?" Mo Xiaoxuan asked, "Is twice-cooked pork considered vegetarian?"

"Yeah, any dish with vegetables can be considered vegetarian. Besides, if you look at a plate of twice-cooked pork, there aren't many meat pieces," Qin Lang explained.

A slightly disdainful expression appeared on the waiter's face, and Mo Xiaoxuan also felt a bit embarrassed. Qin Lang's words were a bit confusing, and he always seemed to profit himself at the expense of the restaurant. But from what she knew through WeChat, his family's financial situation was not bad. Could he be testing me?

"That's enough." Mo Xiaoxuan suggested, "That's it."

"We haven't ordered soup yet!" Qin Lang indulgently looked at her, "Girls should drink more soup."

Mo Xiaoxuan looked at the colorful soup in the picture. The soup in this restaurant is very unique, and different soups are paired with different colors and shapes of tableware, making it look even more tempting.

"This one. Li's Pear Soup," Mo Xiaoxuan

pointed to the cheapest soup on the menu.

“It's a special dish,” the waiter smiled at Mo Xiaoxuan, “Our Pear Soup is slow-cooked over low heat, with a velvety taste and a sweet and fragrant aroma. We have many repeat customers who come back for it every day.”

“Then add it. It's also reasonably priced,”Mo Xiaoxuan politely smiled at the waiter.

“Is it really good?” Qin Lang furrowed his brows again. “A pot of Pear Soup costs 38 yuan. Do you know how much the pears are in the market per kilogram?”

Mo Xiaoxuan's smile was awkwardly frozen, and the waiter remained silent.

“It's not about the price but the unfair price, darling. I'm really angry,” Qin Lang turned to the waiter again. “Isn't there a complimentary soup? Kelp and Egg Soup. It's also nutritious.”

“That is available for orders over 288 yuan.”

“Give us one first. We haven't finished ordering

yet, and besides, we will become repeat customers in the future. Isn′t it worth giving us a complimentary soup?"

"Alright, sir. I will apply for it for you."

Qin Lang nodded in satisfaction, his shrewd eyes rolling in his sockets. He rubbed his chin with his hand and smiled as he looked at Mo Xiaoxuan′s face.

"Darling, is there anything else you want? Don′t be deceived by these waiters. I understand their little tricks the best."

"Okay. That′s enough," Mo Xiaoxuan turned her head to admire the scenery outside, trying to suppress the discomfort in her mind.

"How can that be enough? It′s our first meal outside. Others will regard me as a penny pincher if you do so."

The waiter rolled his eyes to the side. A bitter smile tugged at the corners of Mo Xiaoxuan′s mouth.

"Let′s have a dessert," Qin Lang pointed to the cheapest chocolate parfait on the menu. The smooth chocolate chips lay quietly on top of the white cream, exuding a creamy aroma in the picture. “What′s this?”

“It′s a Chocolate Parfait, Sir,” the waiter patiently smiled.

“Don′t I know its name?” Qin Lang also rolled his eyes, “I am asking about the ingredients.”

“Sorry, I am not sure.”

“Not sure? Well, let me tell you. This is made with Mylikes and Bright Ice Cream. Those three Mylikes are worth a few cents, and the cost of ice cream doesn′t exceed 5 yuan. Yet, you′re charging 28 yuan for it. Isn′t it a robbery? Are you serious?”

The waiter smiled and remained silent, while Mo Xiaoxuan felt a bit cold. She wondered if the air conditioning was set at a lower temperature, as the previous stuffiness had completely dissipated.

“Well, forget it. It′s not necessary,” the smile has disappeared from Mo Xiaoxuan′s face. If this was truly a test, it was going a bit too far. What if he had been lying to me, and his family conditions aren't that good?

"No. How could that be? Girls like you always want something sweet after a meal."

"You seem to know girls well," Mo Xiaoxuan said casually.

Qin Lang seemed to realize he had said too much and smiled awkwardly, "No. Though I haven't eaten any pork, but ...?"

"Fine. Forget it. It's okay. Never mind."

"Darling, you're so considerate. How about having a meal at here and eating dessert at the next store? Girls like you have small appetites, or else you won't be able to eat later."

"You're really attentive," Mo Xiaoxuan smiled with her eyes and eyebrows, her mouth showing a touch of disdain. She had already heard the words "girls like you" five times.

"That's right. Glad you like it. Okay, that's it," Qin Lang handed the menu to the waiter, who mechanically repeated the order.

"We didn′t order rice." Qin Lang added.

"The rice is for free," the waiter said, "Just let us know if you′d like some."

"Free! Then bring us a bowl."

Mo Xiaoxuan felt like she was about to faint. She wanted to leave the scene quickly, but this wasn′t a blind date, he was already her husband. She began to force a smile, and Qin Lang thought she was very happy, which made him even more excited, shouting at the waiter.

"What′s the matter, Sir? Go and arrange the rice quickly. Are you unhappy cause customers like your rice?"

The waiter left, and Mo Xiaoxuan felt there was nothing more to say. They exchanged remarks without really connecting. The dishes arrived, and Qin Lang attentively served various dishes to Mo Xiaoxuan. After they finished eating, Qin Lang looked at the menu and furrowed his brow again.

“The price...”

“I′ve already paid.” Mo Xiaoxuan put away her phone.

“What? How did you pay?”

“There is a QR code on the table.”

“You act so fast. Today is our first date. It′s unreasonable for you to pay this bill.”

“Let′s okay. We′re family now.”

We will live together in the future after all. Anyway, Qin Lang′s family owned a house. The richer a person is, the more stingy he will be. Maybe he was testing me. Mo Xiaoxuan thought in mind.

“You′re so kind,” Qin Lang said, “I would have ordered the Chocolate Parfait and that fish if I had known this. My dear, you′re really good at making money.”

As they left the restaurant, Mo Xiaoxuan prepared to hail a taxi home.

“Wait, darling, you forgot about dessert. It′s my turn to be the host.”

“Oh, yeah. The dessert place next door. Let′s go.”

Mo Xiaoxuan thought to herself that he really knows about these things. It seems he was testing me. I knew he wouldn′t be so stingy. As she turned around, a convenience store stood near the restaurant, and the sun shone brightly. Love seemed to be scorched under its rays.

4.Cohabitation life

"So, did you really decide to divorce? Just because of his stinginess?"

"Do you think it's just an ordinary stinginess? Let me show you what true eccentricity is," Mo Xiaoxuan continued to describe her husband's unusual behavior to me.

Qin Lang had a special hobby—collecting trash. His mother was a university professor and his father was a businessman. Everything Mo Xiaoxuan said about his "good conditions" was true. Despite such a good family background, he really loved collecting trash.

"Garbage" can be seen in every corner of Qin Lang's house. A stack of empty mineral water bottles, worn-out cardboard boxes, and little bundles of tissues scattered around. She even suspected that he had picked up those tissues from restaurants, imagining Qin Lang sneaking them into his pockets at the restaurant. Mo Xiaoxuan felt a mix of anger and amusement at the thought.

Mo Xiaoxuan hadn′t personally witnessed him rummaging through garbage bins, but there was one incident. Qin Lang had claimed that he was going to play basketball, so Mo Xiaoxuan thought of going to see him and bring him a bottle of water. She had never before taken the initiative to bring water to a boy on the basketball court in her youth, and the thought made her feel sweet. With that in mind, she eagerly hurried to the basketball court to visit him. As she approached the basketball court from afar, Mo Xiaoxuan saw Qin Lang. He wasn′t playing basketball. Instead, he was swaying back and forth, looking around. He was holding something in his hand. What could it be? Mo Xiaoxuan′s curiosity was piqued. She rubbed her eyes and focused intently.

She squinted her eyes, trying to strain to see. As she got closer to Qin Lang, she could clearly make out what he was holding—it was an iron pot. She couldn´t believe her eyes, but as she got closer, she confirmed that Qin Lang was indeed holding an iron pot. Unaware of her presence, he continued swaying outside the basketball court´s wire mesh, holding the pot as if it were a treasured weapon accompanying him on his adventures. He swung the pot while anxiously scanning his surroundings, like a serious yet aimless scavenger. Suddenly, he spotted Mo Xiaoxuan approaching. His body stiffened, surprise evident in his eyes. He nervously hid the pot behind him.

"Wow, you, why are you here?" He stuttered when he got nervous.

"Where did this come from?" Mo Xiaoxuan stared at the rusty and mottled iron pot.

"Ah-ha?" he didn´t tell the truth and tried desper ately to wriggle out of giving a clear answer.

At that moment, an inexplicable chill swept over Mo Xiaoxuan's heart: Is this the man I married? She felt like she was submerged in a sea of despair.

"Don't get divorced on impulse as long as he's not stingy with you. After all..." I said.

"He typically stingy with me."

In terms of buying food and cooking, Qin Lang insisted on the principle of one person being responsible for one thing. One time, after Mo Xiaoxuan finished eating at a restaurant, Qin Lang happened to come to pick her up. At that time, Mo Xiaoxuan said to her husband, "Darling, go and pay the bill." As a result, Qin Lang was taken aback and his voice raised several octaves.

"Why should I pay the bill!"

He stood up. His face turned red with anger. His action attracted everyone's attention. Mo Xiaoxuan felt extreme shame. But she still suppressed her anger and grievance, quietly went to the front desk, and paid the bill herself.

“Well. I′m absolutely certain, I can′t bear it for another minute.” She was about to scream on the other end of the phone, “You don′t know how much more outrageous he can be.”

They made a joint agreement to delete all social media apps and dating accounts together. Two weeks later, while Mo Xiaoxuan checked Qin Lang′s phone, she discovered that his account was still intact and logged in. What′s more, there were over 20 girls leaving him messages. When she scrolled through his phone contacts, she found many strange names with vulgar and explicit nicknames. One day, out of curiosity, Mo Xiaoxuan decided to call one of the contacts, and it turned out to be a girl who complained about Qin Lang harassing her and asked him not to call her again. Upon learning all of this, Mo Xiaoxuan naturally started a quarrel. She couldn′t tolerate any deceptive behaviors, but Qin Lang had a quick temper and refused to back down. He insisted that those girls were just friends. **Facing someone**

pretending to be asleep, Mo Xiaoxuan not only wanted to wake him up but also wanted to preach and influence him. The first step for a woman to fall into the abyss is to think she can save a man. Being a saint seems to be an inherent nature of every woman. But Qin Lang refused to admit it. As Mo Xiaoxuan′s anger escalated, he even became physically abusive. One time, he held the back of a knife against her neck. Mo Xiaoxuan was instantly terrified, and afterward, Qin Lang playfully explained to himself that he was using the back of the knife, not the blade, which is enough to show his love to her.

"There′s something even more outrageous," she continued, and by now we had been on the phone for two hours.

Once, a close friend of Mo Xiaoxuan went to Xiamen from Beijing to visit her. Mo Xiaoxuan let her friend stay overnight at her place. During the day, Mo Xiaoxuan was out for work and her friend was left at home with Qin Lang, a jobless vagrant. Her friend was eating fruit in the room when she heard a knocking sound at the door. It was Qin Lang, who pushed her friend aside and walked straight to the bed, lying down and saying that he wanted to rest there. She was so angry that she picked up her bag and left Xiaoxuan′s house.

Qin Lang is extremely fond of lying, but he was not skilled at it. Once, Mo Xiaoxuan suspected that he had fabricated his educational background, and he became extremely anxious. He raised his voice and shouted, “I swear I didn′t graduate from Sanming University (a vocational college). ”What he said only gave himself away. He unintentionally revealed the actual college from which he graduated.

Since then, Mo Xiaoxuan became even more determined to get a divorce. As she mentioned this, she started crying, and I couldn′t bear to listen anymore. Initially, I thought of advising her to endure, but now I couldn′t help but wish to accompany her to file for divorce. She cried for less than three minutes.

"But I can also understand him," Mo Xiaoxuan suddenly said. "Do you know? Actually, he is quite pitiful."

Oh my goodness! I knew she was going to say that. **Over the years, I have heard countless complaints from my friends, and it always ends with the same line "He is so pitiful." And then comes the forgiveness, the endless cycle of back and forth. What does this have to do with me? Does that mean all the pitiful people in the world are my responsibility? Does every pitiful person have their sins wiped away just because they are pitiful? so what is the prison for?** I had a premonition of what she was going to say next, but I had to follow the process. Even though chickens had come home to roost, I began to listen to the pitiful part of him.

He has severe depression and mild mental illness. He can laugh hysterically for a long time even over a small issue, and his laughter sounds like a scream, close to a roar. With a little training, it becomes dolphin-like sounds. The scream made one wonder if he had never laughed before. Or he can instantly become angry, his mouth forming a line that connects his eye corners, then he curses loudly at the wall. Just when you think his emotions have reached their peak, he instantly reveals a smiling face. The momentary emotional switch caused scalp tingling as if people are immersed in an emotional black hole of irritability and unease.

So Mo Xiaoxuan comprehensively analyzed his family background. In the past half a year, she had become half a psychologist.

Qin Lang′ parents started doing business when he was a child. He was locked at home frequently. Loneliness and autism led him to immerse himself in fantasies, losing the ability to have normal interaction as well as a sense of security. When he was young, he would eagerly wait by the window from morning till night, finally seeing his parents return home full of tiredness. They would then scold him for the mess in the house. His parents had been busy all day and had exhausted their patience, so without hesitation, they vented their emotions toward Qin Lang. With tears in his eyes, he dared not argue back, fearing that if he became angry, his parents would abandon him, as they often threatened. But one day, he realized that his parents′ words were just scares, and he began to live recklessly, without any concerns. He needed his parents, yet he also hated them. He would often persuade Mo Xiaoxuan not to trust her parents. There was even a time when Qin Lang′s mother asked Mo Xiaoxuan to provide her ID photo for some procedures.

"Don′t give it to her," Qin Lang exclaimed in a shrill voice, "What if she uses it for something malicious?"

At first, Mo Xiaoxuan thought Qin Lang was a sick guy. After spending more time with his parents, she began to understand Qin Lang′s suspicion. It′s absolutely an “abnormal” family.

His father and mother didn′t live together, and they were economically independent. His mother was involved in managing innovative and entrepreneurial projects at a university, often taking advantage of various educational funds and not hesitating to share her questionable deeds with her children. She would frequently boast at home about obtaining shares in several start-up companies for free and how much public funds she had acquired. As for his father, he remained indifferent to family affairs and paid no attention to his wife or Qin Lang, as if the child didn′t exist. As a result, the household was under the control of the mother, and her mindset directly influenced the entire family.

“That′s a horrible family!” Mo Xiaoxuan′s voice trembled. “It is said that his father even fell in love with his mother′s sister.”

“Whose sister?” I felt overwhelmed by what I was hearing.

"Qin Lang's aunt. He often tells me that he is the son of his aunt, rather than his mother."

"Have you taken him to a mental hospital?" I felt that this was not just an emotional issue.

"Yes, I did." Mo Xiaoxuan said, "But I couldn't bear it anymore when we arrived. He knelt, cried loudly, begged me like a child, worried about my abandonment."

It was not the only time Qin Lang went to the hospital. Although he actively cooperated with treatment, it failed to take effect. Mo Xiaoxuan began to choke, and I knew she still loved him. **As long as a woman still loved a man, no matter how big a mistake the man made, she would definitely turn back.**

I wondered what the world looked like for Qin Lang, and what a more hopeless ocean Qin Lang's world would be. He couldn't see himself, didn't know where his soul resided. Even if he caught a glimpse of it, he couldn't lift himself out of the depths. When he met Mo Xiaoxuan, he felt a glimmer of hope in his life. While this person couldn't save him from his collapsing world, they could accompany each other in the depths of the sea at least. **In my imagination, Qin Lang's face became distorted, portraying a helpless and pitiful yet detestable devil.**

When Mo Xiaoxuan proposed a divorce, Qin Lang's mother naturally held the converse opinion. She kept scolding her own son and even slapped Qin Lang in front of Mo Xiaoxuan. Witnessing this scene, Mo Xiaoxuan changed her countenance and chose to forgive because of the sincere attitude of Qin Lang's mother. However, Qin Lang was still the same just like in the past. And then, Mo Xiaoxuan learned to go and complain to Qin Lang's mother.

"Don't take offense at him, Xiaoxuan." Qin Lang's mother held her hand and looked at her with a smile. "You don't know how much I like you." She continued with a series of compliments and approval for Mo Xiaoxuan.

Hearing these words, Mo Xiaoxuan was once again deeply moved. She was a person who can be easily persuaded by others.

"At the worst, we can live a life together. Why bother yourself with him? We can treat each other sisters," Qin Lang's mother said with a smile.

Hearing this, tears of gratitude welled up in Mo Xiaoxuan's eyes.

"It's not easy for a woman with a failed marriage to find a partner!" Qin Lang's mother continued with a kindly expression, "Besides if you have children in the future, we will educate them well. As your mother-in-law, I'll wholeheartedly help you take care of them. They will be brought up in the right way definitely."

Mo Xiaoxuan nodded, feeling somewhat comforted.

"You see, I've been thinking about it," Qin Lang's mother said, holding Mo Xioaxuan's hand while patting her hand back. "Once you have a baby.

20,000 yuan per month is enough for him or her since you and I pay half of the living expenses. And as for the house, the ones we have in our family are not in good locations and are already rented out. Why don't we take out a joint loan and buy a good one in the city center? Since you won 30,000 - 40,000 yuan per month..."

Before she could finish listening, Mo Xiaoxuan moved her hand and fled away from the house. On her way back, tears streamed down her face. She realized that she had fallen into a den of bandits.

At present, she was alone and helpless. People around her don't show any understanding. It hasn't been a month since their marriage, and she proposed a divorce immediately. Everyone around her regards her as insane. Every time she mentioned divorce, Qin Lang would kneel, tears streaming down his face, begging her, and even the entire family seemed ready to kneel before her. This kind-hearted girl couldn't withstand such moral coercion and reluctantly compromised. That compromise lasted for six months, but for her, it felt like a lifetime of endless darkness.

During this period, Mo Xiaoxuan discovered that Qin Lang had an ex-wife. She wasn′t shocked upon receiving this news at the beginning. Even one day, after a serious argument with Qin Lang, she couldn′t take it anymore. She retrieved the phone number that she saved secretly previously, and called his ex-wife.

"I advise you to be patient," the ex-wife said on the other end of the phone in a calm tone. "He is easy to be persuaded. Don′t take his words seriously. You just need to appease him when he is angry. Look at his mental status, how long do you think he can live? What′s more, he is impotent although he chats up girls everywhere." The ex-wife let out a cold laugh over the phone. "So, I advise you to be patient. Once he passes away, all his property will be yours. Don′t follow in my footsteps. Ah! It was precisely because I couldn′t bear him anymore, I had an affair and out of this game. I believe in you, come on."

It turned Mo Xiaoxuan's world upside down. Since then, she made up her mind that she must divorce, or she would be burnt out by the family.

Yet, every time she mentioned divorce, he would plead and she would be softhearted. The closest still failed. They all arrived at the Civil Affairs Bureau. Qin Lang wore a suit and held a bouquet of roses which was only worth 10 yuan. He knelt once again, with his parents and his mother's students behind him, collectively begging her not to divorce. Mo Xiaoxuan's compassionate heart couldn't withstand such a bombardment, and she surrendcred once again.

On a sunny Sunday afternoon, Mo Xiaoxuan couldn't find a valuable necklace and went to hurl a question at Qin Lang.

"I didn't take it." Qin Lang's eyes darted around, avoiding direct eye contact. Without a word, Mo Xiaoxuan went upstairs and started rummaging through chests and cupboards to find the necklace.

"What are you doing?" Qin Lang roared.

Ignoring this roar, Mo Xiaoxuan kept searching for the necklace but failed. Then, she opened a drawer next to the computer desk, numerous necklaces appear in awe. It′s filled with jewelry. Rings, necklaces, and earrings were scattered in it. Mo Xiaoxuan was stunned.

"Where did you get all these things?" Mo Xiaoxuan asked.

Qin Lang rushed up to Mo Xiaoxuan like a monkey and closed the drawer. "Who let you do this!"

"How did you get so many jewelry? Did you steal them?"

It may be because of the sensitive vocabulary "steel", Qin Lang became flustered:"I didn′t steal them. These are all from my ex-girlfriends."

Under questioning, Mo Xiaoxuan finally understood that Qin Lang was not a guy who was only stingy with himself. He would even ask for the return of jewelry he had given to his ex-girlfriends as well as the wedding ring from his ex-wife.

Mo Xiaoxuan couldn't take it anymore. Although she didn't find the necklace, she reached the breaking point. The pent-up anger overwhelmed her, and she slapped Qin Lang twice. Surprisingly, Qin Lang retaliated and hit her back twice. Mo Xiaoxuan was shattered, and she started crying uncontrollably. Instead of consoling her, Qin Lang impatiently told her to leave. She continued crying and refused to go. Qin Lang began dragging her out of the house, and Mo Xiaoxuan resisted. He held onto her tightly and dragged her from the second floor to the first floor, and then outside, closing the front door. Mo Xiaoxuan stood outside, bruised and crying, but no one paid attention to her.

Since then, she experienced frequent domestic violence.

She stayed in the pit of despair just like that,

blaming others for not saving her. But how could they save her? Every time she decided to leave, she would return for pity, moral pressure, and unwillingness. The cycle repeated dozens of times. On one day, she called me and said she did want to divorce, and they were now separated since legal intervention had taken place.

Finally, I saw a glimmer of hope.

5.The Path of Despair

Six months later, Mo Xiaoxuan came to Shanghai from Xiamen again. I could see that she looked much better. I thought she had resolved the divorce issue.

"Not yet, we have come to a deadlock." She said without sadness on her face. I guessed that she might have become somewhat numb.

"What! Is he still harassing you or what?"

Then she began recounting the long journey of divorce over the past six months.

"I just want to run out of her time." His is Qin Lang and his lawyer′s attitude. Either get or destroy it. He agreed to divorce his ex-wife two years after applying.Regarding Mo Xiaoxuan, it all depended on his mood. Mo Xiaoxuan tried to appeal the injustice in court, but the law didn′t provide much protection for her. To make matters worse, Qin Lang′s mother happened to be a law professor—a well-educated gangster family. Mo Xiaoxuan was stripped of the opportunity to surrender.

During that period, Mo Xiaoxuan almost suffered from depression. Legally, she couldn′t get a penny, and the divorce agreement wouldn′t take effect as long as Qin Lang refused to sign it. So Mo Xiaoxuan sought help everywhere, consulting lawyers and feeling helpless and as insignificant as dust. Giving charcoal in the snow is rare in this society. Most people prefer to add to the success of others, while some enjoy pouring fuel on the fire. Mo Xiaoxuan′s marriage was already hard-pressed, but she didn′t receive much sympathy from the surrounding people. Suddenly, there were many experienced "guides" appearing out of nowhere. Some wanted to introduce her to influential locals, offering her a sense of reliance. Mo Xiaoxuan met one of these "locals" who were old and repulsive, and she felt it was more like a sacrifice—jumping from one fire pit to another. Therefore, Mo Xiaoxuan politely declined the help.

One of her friends was an artist who was very open-minded. This friend began to brainwash Mo Xiaoxuan, saying that everything in her life was the same as the unmarried period. The only difference is a certificate. when the time comes, she will take Mo Xiaoxuan to the Civil Affairs Bureau and get this divorce certificate. Everything is as before. Hence, Mo Xiaoxuan took this to be true. She drank with this friend every day at bars. At first, Mo Xiaoxuan enjoyed this kind of numbing effect, but later she realized that her state of mind was getting worse, and her emotions were becoming more unstable. I advised Mo Xiaoxuan to run and think more when she had nothing to do. I also sent her a sports bracelet, but she didn′t want to exercise. She preferred to quietly stay alone in a state of despair and sadness because she felt it was safer that way. Some people suggested that she read books, but she said she couldn′t concentrate.

Someone advised her to talk to her family, but she thought it would bring shame to her family. Even though she deeply regretted it, she hadn't told her family about her marriage until now. She felt that she was too ashamed and didn't want her family to bear the same pressure as her. Therefore, she planned to take on everything by herself before informing her family.

She was not cowardly, but rather trapped in her pain. During this period, Qin Lang didn't stop bothering her for a moment. On one hand, he continued to flirt with other women. On the other hand, he sent messages trying to win Mo Xiaoxuan back. Her empathy slowly turned into numbness, and all she wanted in the end was a divorce. His actions (like a sick chameleon, kneeling and begging her at times, violently assaulting her like a demon at other times, and displaying a child-like dependence on her) all seemed like a charade in her eyes.

I suddenly realized that in this society, the

strong are often aggressors who are skilled at depriving and invading others. They are great pretenders, attracting prey and devouring them alive in the guise of being well-educated. Everyone says that society has evolved, but it has always been governed by the law of the jungle, with players changing one after another, packaged in different shells.

With the help of a kind-hearted lawyer, she finally liberated herself from the marriage a year later. Throughout that year, Qin Lang continued to harass her, but she managed to resist the temptation to return.

On the day of their divorce, Qin Lang clung to the door of the taxi, kneeling on the ground and begging her. It was on Christmas Eve.

"I will buy you an apple, okay?" he begged her like a child as if the apple was an incredible gift.

"There's something wrong with you!"

Exerting all her strength, Mo Xiaoxuan kicked

Qin Lang who was clinging to the door. The helplessness, endurance, hatred, sympathy, despair, hope, conflicting struggles of love and hate and unrealized fantasies and realities in the past year were all kicked away just like Qin Lang. The car door slammed shut with a loud "bang." Mo Xiaoxuan headed forward, seating in the tax, and recalled the day of their marriage. She was sitting coyly with him in a taxi that day, but now, she kicked him, the ex-husband away. She suddenly felt it was ridiculous. She laughed while tears formed in her eyes.

The bride was smiling last year here,

While crying at the same place at this moment.

The desolation of the world formed a transparent barrier in front of her eyes, dissipating into vapor at the slightest touch. It was followed by a gushing stream of tears. She had finally learned to be indifferent to pleas, and she had become determined and strong.

"You heartless girl!" The intrusive driver

grumbled indignantly. "The boy is so pitiful. Why don't you give him another chance?"

"Shut up! Focus on your own business!" Mo Xiaoxuan shouted at the driver, her tears breaking free despite her words.

Pity and hatred cannot cancel each other out, just as merits and faults cannot offset each other. They merely bury each other, coexisting in parallel. When one side departs, the other takes the stage. As members of society, we must always bear these contradictions.

At the Christmas Eve party, a group of friends awaited Mo Xiaoxuan, congratulating her on escaping from the devil's talons. However, she couldn't tell whom the talons belong to—Qin Lang's family, her inner turmoil, or the intangible webcast over women by the gloomy sky. It's no way to know.

She was thankful to be free!

6.Light of Hope

After experiencing 3-day flash marriage and a 3-year dispute, she was single again. Even though she was not yet 30 years old, her value in the marriage market has been directly reduced by 50%. Divorced women are inexplicably criticized and difficult to marry. After the divorce, Mo Xiaoxuan went on blind dates again and truly experienced the pain of a woman with a failed marriage. Age-appropriate young boys would nitpick on her condition. The roles have changed. Property, job, salary, and everything else are inquired. However, as long as hearing about the second marriage, they paid the bill and went away.

One of her friends was a teacher, she suggested Mo Xiaoxuan find another man. With a backup, she can compete in the face of Qin Lang. Otherwise, she would be alone and helpless. It would be a hard case once Qin Lang find her. Naturally, the friend introduced Mo Xiaoxuan to a director from the Construction Bureau. However, Mo Xiaoxuan returned after only having a partial meal with the director, who was about to enter aging.

"How can you still be picky?" the friend found it unbelievable. "You are going to have a second marriage. Finding someone like him is quite well in the marriage market. Besides, he has never been married before," her friend raised an eyebrow and smirked. "Moreover, he has a fat job. How many girls try to connect with him enthusiastically?" By implication, as a divorced woman with a set of problems, Mo Xiaoxuan should accept her fate. Destiny wouldn't treat her unfairly.

But in Mo Xiaoxuan's eyes, she had never truly enjoyed married life at all, which was too unfair. For her, there was no difference between marriage and single states. While she was categorized as a married woman-in-law. This added a sense of injustice and grievance to her.

She went to school to teach, feeling that everyone was gossiping about her behind her back. Walking down the street, she couldn′t lift her head. During that period, she was on the verge of depression once again. She resisted the fact of her divorce in her heart. If she could turn back time to that afternoon, she would never have gone to the Civil Affairs Bureau with that person. She had never expected that an impulsive marriage would bring her tremendous pressure and a significant change in her mindset. At such a young age, she had lost much of her vitality and enthusiasm, appearing like a gloomy sunset. But every day, she had to dress herself up neatly because a bunch of people around were waiting to see her jokes. At school, her colleagues would smile at her, but their eyes seemed mocking. Some even made sympathetic sounds with their mouths. She pretended not to see, but with each experience of such a scene, her heart bore a scar.

Under the instigation of those unreliable friends, she once again began incessantly going on blind dates.

Young people in modern life have a hollow optimism, as if recklessly moving forward is a force that can erase the mess and wreckage of the past, but it is merely an escape from the unbearable past and reality.

Mo Xiaoxuan is, after all, an independent woman with a good job, wealth, and beauty in the new era. Even though, people in Xiamen don′t care about that. If you′re divorced and don′t have a local household registration, you′re essentially powerless. I′m often amazed by the mindset of some developed regions. Look at the city with its tall buildings, dazzling lights, and glamorous people coming in and out of theaters and shopping malls, their thinking is still stuck in a hundred years ago, unable to appreciate any beauty or adventurous spirit that goes beyond tradition.

I can no longer tell if material development is too fast or spiritual development is too slow.

Even my friends are the same. They advised me not to associate with Mo Xiaoxuan, fearing that she might have a negative influence on me. I remain indifferent to my mother′s attitude, but this indifference deeply hurts me. Does everyone want to keep away from the weak avoiding getting caught in bad luck? Where should we flee to if I am a weak someday or now, or if the reader who is reading my work is a weak? In the vast ocean of people, the walls constructed by the indifference of others have left all kindness and faith lost in the distant sky. The strong are overbearing, and the weak deceive each other. This is the reality of the human world.

"I bought a house."

A whole year after her divorce, I received her call again.

I didn′t know how she managed to get through

the whole year. I often saw her Moments showing pictures of enjoying life. In her words, so many people were waiting to see her downfall, and she couldn′t let them have their way. Even if she cried at midnight, she would wear a mask of a sweet smile the next day. She would indulge in excessive eating and then undergo liposuction to lose weight. Despite the extreme methods, she was still striving to maintain her dignity. As long as one knows how to uphold their dignity, they won′t collapse. Even if the methods are foolish and bring them to the brink of death. Despite enduring countless nights of despair, she miraculously resurrected herself. Although the methods were dull and on the brink of death, she miraculously revived after enduring those desperate nights.

"I used to be too lacking in love and too in need of companionship from a man, that′s why I was always soft-hearted."

One day, Xiaoxuan returned to her hometown

and played the piano in the living room. The melody was serene and melancholic. Xiaoxuan′s long hair often cascaded down, giving her a sorrowful yet captivating appearance. Her mother watched her from the side, tears welled up in her eyes, and she suddenly went up to hug her.

"Xuan, I′ve heard your story." With that, Xiaoxuan′s mother embraced her and started crying. Xiaoxuan was startled, hearing her mother′s sobs, she didn′t lift her head, burying it deeply in her mother′s chest, tears silently soaking her mother′s clothes. From childhood, she had been carefully nurtured by her family, hoping to step into a bright future. Unfortunately, this exhaustive cultivation failed to bring her marital happiness. Perhaps the excellence of a woman is exactly a paradox in the rules of marriage. It was thought to be an extra point for happiness but turned out to be a sacrificial offering to marriage. How could Xiaoxuan learn to summarize it? She began to sob loudly. They snuggled up together. This marriage has caused irreparable harm to this ordinary family.

The family provided the down payment and helped her buy a house in Xiamen. Now, she only needs to make monthly mortgage payments.

She used to look for men with good economic conditions and owned many houses. But now, she wanted to have a house of her own. After losing many precious things in life, she decided to grasp her own happiness, the one that came from herself instead of others, regardless it was material or spiritual. She strives to sprinkle more sunlight into her life through a beam of light, revitalizing the chaotic past.

"Even if I, Mo Xiaoxuan, were single for a lifetime, I won′t be scared anymore."

At this moment, I feel that she′s shining brightly. My friend, Mo Xiaoxuan, is not a highly intelligent person. She lives straightforwardly and sometimes goes too far in her efforts, but she cannot tolerate a dull life. She has come from the storms and endured the hardships. Finally, through tears and blood, she has learned that true independence comes from inner confidence, rather than external so-called "good conditions."

Another year passed, Mo Xiaoxuan went to Russia to pursue a doctoral degree in piano. Upon returning, she earned a six-figure annual salary. She not only overcame the damage caused by that man but also dealt a blow to society′s prejudice against her. From a chaotic wasteland, she built a shining and successful career tower.

It′s so unfair to bind a woman′s achievements to her marriage! It′s incredibly unfair and ridiculous!

A woman′s success in marriage, yes, can be seen as an achievement. But an unsuccessful marriage shall not be classified as a failure in life. As society won′t judge a man′s future by a failed startup. Similarly, a woman′s failed marriage should not be completely negated. The sun rises

and sets, casting its impartial radiance upon everyone. Even in the most desolate places, there is resilient life surging forth. Every individual should have the chance to start anew.

I believe that this article is not just written for women, but for countless ordinary people who have gone through trials and tribulations. We cannot choose where we are born, but we can choose how we live our lives. I sincerely hope that both my readers and I can face life with the same courage as Mo Xiaoxuan.

Mo Xiaoxuan finally achieved success. She is a hero herself.